DATE DUE

1979			
1			

AROUND THE EDGE OF WAR

AROUND THE EDGE OF WAR

JOHN FORTH AMORY

*A New Approach
to the Problems
of American
Foreign Policy*

Clarkson N. Potter, Inc./Publisher

NEW YORK

Library of Congress Catalogue Card Number: 61-17877

MANUFACTURED IN THE UNITED STATES OF AMERICA BY

BOOK CRAFTSMEN ASSOCIATES, INC., NEW YORK

First Edition

. . . to Caipe . . .

Contents

FOREWORD

The fact that you are reading these words is reasonable proof that the nuclear barrier is still in place against direct war between the United States and the Soviet Union. Otherwise, you and several hundred million Americans, Russians, Chinese, Europeans and others would be dead. From this very basic standpoint the existence of the barrier is a blessing; but it also presents extraordinary problems for the makers and shapers of American foreign policy.

The military stalemate, obliged by effective nuclear parity, implies that within delicate limits the United States and the Soviet Union must and do make use of new or secondary methods of policy enforcement in those world areas where the power conflict that characterizes these decades is carried on, with increasing tenseness, by the two great antagonists. American foreign policy and the available instruments for its enforcement thus assume far more importance than ever before in our history; we can no longer trust to luck or superior military force to put our policies into effect, even when they are not suitable. Correctness in foreign policy, certainty that it serves the interests of the nation as a whole, and application of policy in line with existing facts, not wishful thinking, are no longer matters for improvisation, in which errors can be made with impunity.

In a period of military stalemate, when we and the enemy dare not bring determinant weapons into play, the safety of the nation comes to depend on secondary methods of policy enforcement, to checkmate or overbalance the antagonist on many small fronts, which, nevertheless, in their totality, can lead just as surely to victory or defeat as all-out war.

One purpose of *Around the Edge of War* is to help Americans think about these secondary methods, which may be nontraditional, and to stir people into wondering why, in so many crises, our methods of policy enforcement have proved impotent against the countermethods used by the Soviet Union. We have approached this analysis from the premise that to man-made problems man can find answers.

Another purpose is to lead Americans to consideration of the new and special circumstances in which our methods of policy enforcement must operate, particularly the environment of "upheaval," which characterizes the vast belt of underdeveloped areas around the world, the main arena of conflict for the United States and the Soviet Union. In these key areas, where great submerged majorities are rising, the future of the United States may be determined. It is there that American policy, both pragmatically and morally, has been most erroneous; and it is there, too, that the Soviet Union has gained many small victories that go, one by one, into the totality. We shall examine, not the surface characteristics of the "upheaval areas," which our policymakers know well enough, but the upheaval itself, the movement of submerged peoples, its social, military and ideological nature, which our policy-makers, so far, have given no indication of understanding. We shall examine, too, the instruments of policy formation and policy enforcement that the United States has made use of in the upheaval areas, and shall do so in a spirit of frank, basic and, hopefully, constructive criticism.

Our primary purpose, of course, is to help Americans think about our foreign policy as a whole, about how it is made, whence derived, and whether it has been right or wrong in terms of the whole national interest and pragmatically in terms of results. We want especially to lead Americans to think of people, of men, women and children; for we believe that in this period of military stalemate the only remaining weapons that can be used, for or against us, are the people of the earth, whom Jefferson defined as the only legitimate source of power—the great majorities who, after millennia, are coming into their own. We think that the safety of the United States, the moral health of the American people and the survival of our national freedoms depend on whether we go with this swelling tide of people or against it.

Millions of words have been written in the past few years explaining, criticizing, expounding, praising or agonizingly reappraising all the surfaces of American foreign policy. The experts have peered over and over again at our policies from every side except one; they have not looked *inside*. We propose to do so. We propose to examine especially the most taboo of all subjects concerning American foreign policy, the key and increasingly fatal role of our overseas investor group. Readers may find our views somewhat different from the editorials in the daily newspapers or the national-circulation magazines; to adjust to this difference, we suggest they try the inventor's trick of looking at a thing newly, of seeing the customary cup with two handles instead of one, or the habitual chair with three to five legs instead of four. Our hope is to provoke original thought, a main missing element in American policy formation, as it is in American life generally in this particular era.

We shall deliberately confine this analysis to conditions, means, content and objectives of American policy which policy-shapers, if they will, can control; and with equal deliberation we shall ignore many headlined points of contention with the Soviet Union—Berlin, Nuclear Test Ban, Disarmament and the like—over which policy-shapers have no control. On these topics, the United States or the Soviet Union may pronounce any policies, good or bad, they choose; but they cannot enforce those policies against each other except by mutual agreement, short of suicidal war. Therefore the areas of maneuver for the United States, in this period of nuclear parity, are rigidly limited to those areas where direct military conflict with the Soviet Union is not involved. Those are the areas in which a corrected American foreign policy could be applied victoriously; they are, therefore, the primary ones we should concern ourselves with in the formation and application of foreign policy for this period of stalemate.

Many preconditioned readers, and certainly all the experts whose advice America has so far taken in formation of foreign policy, will condemn the analysis presented in *Around the Edge of War*. That, if honestly done, is their privilege. We ask only that they come up with a better analysis, and that they do so soon. The emergency is now.

All power is inherent in the people.

—Thomas Jefferson

PART 1

NEW LEVERAGE OF POWER

Global warfare contains now
only the germs of double suicide.
— *Gen. Douglas MacArthur*

Phrase repeated in speeches in New York, Lansing, Michigan, and Manila, June-July, 1961.

1

Hydrogen Bomb or Tomahawk?

For many years American foreign policy was based on a dream of unchallenged world power, a dream in which America, by waving a nuclear wand, could keep the world's little people safe against the rising menace of the Soviet Union. Our military, economic and propaganda instrumentalities of foreign policy reflected the dream all too clearly, as did the thin threads of alliance, strengthened somewhat by an endless flow of dollars, which we spun out of nuclear cocoons. Successive American leaders used magic incantations, such as "massive retaliation," to ward off the enemy; and gambling on an open-card ace, they took calculated risks in a new variety of poker called "brinkmanship."

A little late, the dream began to fade in the face of reality, although some of the fantasy, only too obviously, lingered on. There was an almost abrupt realization that the Soviet Union also had missiles with nuclear warheads capable of incalculable destruction; and simultaneously there arose a degree of doubt about the strength of our paper alliances. Here and there occasional questions were asked, some of them rather pointed. Why was the United States, the most powerful nation on earth, consistently on the losing side in the world tug-of-cold-war? As small loss added to small loss and the total grew, our military forces became still more potent, our stockpile of bombs expanded, our bases girdled the globe. Yet, side by side with these, side by side with our superintelligence network, our far-flung information services and our expensive allies, our small losses in the field of foreign policy continued to mount. What was wrong?

There was an understandable reluctance to face the facts after such a lengthy period of presumed superiority and world leadership; but the facts were clear, and slowly came into focus: There were two world power centers, not just one; and both had nuclear weapons of total destruction in amounts sufficient to guarantee that neither side could achieve factual, as opposed to numerical, superiority. Since there could be no victory in vaporization of both sides, it became plain that the temporary American dream of being an unchallenged world power, with little basis at any time, no longer had any basis at all. Another fact thus became clear, although it has still not been widely recognized on the popular level and has been carefully ignored by most commentators: For the time being, within the

4

limits of a hair-trigger balance, large-scale nuclear warfare had negated itself.

In these conditions of stalemate between the two antagonists, the rattling of hydrogen bombs or multi-megaton missiles became a rather poor bluff, of rapidly diminishing value even for propaganda purposes. In a condition of nuclear stand-off, the United States and the Soviet Union, aware that any direct conflict could lead to mutual destruction, sought other forms of more or less indirect conflict, other ways of imposing their respective policies.

Meanwhile, each kept careful watch on the other, fearing a breakthrough into some new area, perhaps some defictionalized version of a force field impervious to missiles, that would upset the technological balance and leave one power destroyed and the other the ruler of the world; fearing, too, the unpredictable error, the incalculable human element, which could touch off Armageddon. The delicate balance, however, continued; and, for the time being, nuclear warfare, on a determinant scale, could not enter practically into calculations of global strategy by either side. A key power base for American foreign policy had been, at least temporarily, eliminated. In its place, we had no substitute; but the Soviet Union, with considerable agility, discovered one.

Even during the dream, when America's policy-makers were most deeply withdrawn from unpalatable reality, a few restless sleepers here and there wakened to wonder. Taking out paper and pencil, they reckoned that one hydrogen bomb could vaporize x millions of men, women and children; but they were stumped when they tried to calculate how many hydrogen bombs would be needed to vaporize one dozen armed men in an unknown hideout. The problem was also put in another way: On the man-to-man level, which is the deadlier weapon, a hydrogen bomb or a tomahawk? It was also observed that the purpose of war, as the textbooks duly note, is to impose by force a policy which cannot be imposed otherwise; imposition of policy is the end; war is merely the means.

A suspicion gradually grew, both in the United States and the Soviet Union, that the large-scale nuclear weapons had created a confusion between means and end. Could they have altered the very objectives of war? How is that objective attained through hydrogenocide? With the nuclear stand-off, the questions were still, fortunately, in abeyance; but it seemed clear that, except for purposes of world suicide, warfare with all-destructive weapons would be less effective in achieving the primary objectives of war than with bows and arrows. It has been seriously suggested that if the United States were to rely solely on large-scale nuclear weapons for its defense, a few dozen resurrected Roman legions with short swords could sweep through the country, and that old J.E.B. Stuart, come back from Valhalla, could easily blitz Fort Knox.

Unfortunately, the realization of these facts came late to the United States; we clung to our atomic symbol like a child to its first teddy-bear. Meanwhile, several hundred million people in a dozen lands moved toward the Soviet Union. With our nuclear terror masks hanging over their heads, Red Chinese ground troops overran Chiang Kai-shek and MacArthur; Ho Chi Minh's "little brown men" wiped out grizzled German veterans in France's Foreign Legion; underfed Laotians easily defeated the overfed ones on our side; a few hundred bearded Cubans eliminated 12,000 picked Batista troops, trained and fully equipped by Uncle Sam; and around the world anti-Yankee rioters purpled the air with insults.

How could a foreign policy based on a nonusable weapon be applied? Obviously, it could not; nuclear threat to enforce American policy, whether directed against the Soviet Union or the least of our opponents, became pointless, apart from the primary image of horror it evoked. Yet, equally obviously, the realities of a savage world made American policy, however correct, largely impotent without power behind it, without a leverage that could be applied at any given point.

This was the essential power dilemma of the United States, a dilemma that became more perplexing with the negation, not only of large-scale nuclear warfare, but, increasingly, of "conventional" warfare in the classic sense. Fearful of touching off the nuclear holocaust, neither power dared risk a direct military clash of any kind; at each point, whether Berlin or Cuba, where the clash might arise, one side or the other, or both, backed down, with a peculiar regard for each other's "face" that habitual insult and recrimination could not disguise. In many essential ways, this was a new development in human history; it was not surprising, therefore, that a new theory of military and social conflict arose, suitable for conditions of stalemate in nuclear and conventional warfare. The theory, moreover, became practice; and while the new type of conflict may be ephemeral, depending as it does on the hair-trigger balance of nuclear stalemate, it is nonetheless real for the present. Real, too, are the victories it has enabled

7

the Soviet Union to win with no shedding of Russian blood; although it brought death and suffering to hundreds of thousands of the "little peoples" we so wishfully "kept safe," as we thought, back in the days of our nuclear dream.

Until quite recently, American assumption of superior force led the Executive, the Constitutional fountainhead of foreign policy, to haphazard policy formulations; little care or skill was given to basic analysis of problems or their long-range solutions. If, on the spur of the moment, a given objective was decided on in some world area of American interest, it was assumed that it would be attained without difficulty, for the simple reason that no one would dare keep us from it. The first important step by the United States in the direction that was to lead to perennial cold war and, eventually, to our present circumstances, was taken without thought when, at the insistence of exhausted Britain, we took over from her the care and feeding of Greece; nevertheless, the objective—to keep Soviet-influenced partisans, our wartime allies, from taking over the Greek government—was attained. At that time, however, we in fact had superior bases of both military and economic power, effective means of enforcing our policy.

After the nuclear stalemate took shape, a military basis of power for American foreign policy was eliminated, so far as our main opponent was concerned; and the only usable means of policy enforcement left to us became principally economic, means which could not be applied directly against the Soviet Union and had relatively limited fringe value. The two world power

8

centers were placed in the frustrating and somewhat embarrassing position of having no way to get at each other's throats. The United States had no direct means of making its anti-Soviet policy effective; the Soviet Union was equally hamstrung in any attempt at direct imposition of its policy on the United States.

To recover a means of imposing its policy, the United States began establishing a string of weapon bases around the Soviet perimeter, using its economic power, effective there, to obtain base rights from the border countries. The Soviet Union was not a match for the United States, economically, outside its controlled territories, so use of similar economic leverages to make its anti-American policy effective was impossible at the time. It moved instead, first, to counteract the threat of perimeter bases by development of long-range missiles; second, and most significantly, it began effective use of *people* as a power base for its foreign policy.

Faced with the new "people weapon," which we shall examine, American policy came up against defeat after defeat in each area of serious challenge outside of Europe, where a line of demarcation had been set up. Successes in the European areas where the challenge was limited, achieved even there at costs calculated at upward of $70,000 million, helped maintain American official morale; but frustration in the areas of challenge, the vast underdeveloped regions of popular upheaval, led to a degree of retreat by American policy-makers into a make-believe world, in which billions were frantically poured down sand holes in lieu of realistic appraisals and policy construction.

The use of people to "implement" policy had long been a Soviet objective; the idea had been tried out in countless Communist parties, labor organizations and "popular fronts" around the world, with remarkably little success. The reason for the failure, however, lay more in tactics than in the idea itself. The Comintern, Cominform and similar devices had attempted to impose organizations, to set up frameworks artificially and to group people within them for pressure purposes related to Soviet foreign policy. The new Soviet plan, on the contrary, was built around the tactic of going with existing popular trends instead of against them, of penetrating existing movements instead of setting up new ones, and of linking up with legitimate, recognized aspirations instead of importing slogans and issues as obligatory rallying points.

The new tactic began paying off for the Soviet Union immediately. It fitted in exactly with a trend that was becoming a tidal wave, the huge upward movement of the submerged peoples in the underdeveloped countries. It was at this point that American foreign policy became inchoate; and policy-shapers, seeking to counter the Soviet moves, began making the mistakes that led, step by step, to the debacle of the 1960's and the frantic improvisations of policy that took place.

The discovery of the Soviet Union that despite the American checkmate of its military and economic bases of power for policy enforcement, it could make effective use of a relatively unlimited third force, people, provoked the near-collapse in American foreign policy. The two opposing world power centers had checkmated each other militarily at each point of major test; but the new "people force" broke through and put the United States on the defensive. World initiative, even in American preserves such as Latin America, began gradually passing into Soviet hands.

For every other Soviet weapon, military or economic, there are counterbalancing American weapons. For the "people weapon," the United States has so far not devised a counterbalance. A basic problem is that the "people weapon" is not, strictly speaking, in Soviet hands; the huge upheavals of the great masses of people in the underdeveloped lands have taken place without regard for Soviet designs or master plans; the Soviet Union has merely hitched a ride, so to speak. Yet this indirect weapon has upset American foreign policy far more than the nuclear stand-off. Frantic efforts to counterbalance it have been made; but the lack of understanding of its nature has been obvious not only in the theories voiced by our policy-makers, but most pragmatically, in their actions, ending one by one in failure and defeat. It is especially clear in present American efforts—which may be fatally based on a false premise—to counteract the new strategy, indeed, the new ideology, of military and social conflict which, more and more widely, is guiding the peoples in the areas of upheaval.

Before we examine the premise of the present American policy of going against the tide of upheaval, in contrast to the Soviet policy of going with it, let us look at the tide itself, in the special forms it is taking in the underdeveloped lands of Asia, Africa and Latin America.

I am afraid that today we sing too much of arms and neglect the man.

— *Gen. Maxwell D. Taylor*

As quoted in New York Times Magazine; May 7, 1961.

2

People as a Power Base

After the stalemate between the United States and the Soviet Union became apparent, the power bases for enforcement of foreign policy were balanced off; and both nations, in a series of trials and errors, thrusts and counterthrusts—all checkmated, searched for alternatives. The Soviet Union found one. Through the use of people as the new leverage of power, it began to nullify the military and economic superiority of the United States in the earth-wide belt of "upheaval lands," the areas where the great submerged majorities, for the first time in history, were rising slowly or suddenly against their minority rulers and those bound to them, to gather their national destinies into their own hands. Both powers had toyed with the idea of using the new leverage; but the United States, linked through its overseas investors with the minorities, had no way to line up the resentful majorities on its side and at the same time retain the "more practical" loyalties of the "power elite." This dilemma will be explored later; but while the United States was caught in it, the Soviet Union extricated itself from a dilemma of its own and began moving with the upheaval tide and helping move it in turn against the United States.

The dilemma of the Soviet Union, in its initial attempts to make use of people as a power base for its foreign policy, may seem minor to Americans, compared to the dilemma of the United States. For the Russians, as indoctrinated Marxists, it nevertheless was an even more serious problem. Marxism, as it had been interpreted by Russians and Europeans generally, presumed that social change would come about through violent interaction between industrial or finance capitalists, on one side, and the "industrial proletariat," that is, city wage earners, on the other. Peasants at best were considered doubtful allies, to be led by the wage earners. The whole initial period of "socialist construction," according to Marxist thinkers from Marx himself through Lenin and Stalin, was to be under the domination of what was called "the dictatorship of the proletariat." The theory had been borne out in the Russian Revolution, in which Lenin had more trouble overcoming the peasantry than he had in removing capitalists and aristocrats. Stalin continued the battle, which was not finally solved in Russia until victory in World War II, which brought national unity. How then, in the underdeveloped lands, with their small minority of "industrial

13

proletariat," most of them better fed than the average, and with an overwhelming mass of "peasants," could a "people power" be used as a basis for enforcement of Soviet policy against the United States?

The answer was provided by China's Mao Tse-tung, who in the course of an interminable war against Chiang Kai-shek, discovered that the peasants could be used quite easily by the simple procedure of joining them rather than fighting them, helping them build up their organization—and he observed that peasant wars had failed in the past because of lack of organization—and then, little by little, taking over the movement with an indoctrinated corps made up of elite members of any of the out-groups, not necessarily of city wage earners. When Khrushchev came to power in the Soviet Union, as more of a practical man than a theorist, Mao's discovery came up for serious consideration for the first time. Khrushchev made no pontifical Marxist remarks on the subject; but in a short while the Mao approach began to seep as by osmosis into Russian policy toward the regions of upheaval throughout the world. The new theory, adaptable for each such region, was that social change could come about through the organized and armed action of any majority out-group, regardless of its position in the previous Marxist hierarchy of such groups.

This approach immediately made it possible for the Soviet Union, along with China, to take the side of the rising majorities in every underdeveloped country, rather than merely enter into feeble alliances with minority out-groups or concentrate on penetration of the "industrial proletariat," which, in many underdeveloped lands, was a comparative aristocracy. The approach enabled the Soviet Union to present itself as an ally of some two-thirds of the 3,000 million men, women and children—not counting some 90 million babes-in-womb at the moment—inhabiting the earth. That is roughly the division in membership between the "out-groups" and the "in-groups," between the various "power-elites" of the world and the masses of people they control. The alliance, of course, is far from consolidated; the out-group majorities in the upheaval lands, as they organize, have their own ideas, which are not necessarily those of the Soviet Union or China. Events do not move in the same rhythm with plans; and one can imagine the exasperation of a Communist agitator attempting to arouse the out-groups of some backward area with a father-to-son tradition of perhaps a thousand years of sullen resistance to change.

Resistance was, in fact, greater than the Soviet Union had planned for in two types of underdeveloped areas. The Russian planners found that in much of the Moslem world, in Asia and Africa, and on the African continent as a whole, the local populations were far too backward, much too poorly organized, to be used effectively as a weapon against American policy; in other areas, particularly in most of Latin America, they found that the existing governments, either through the use of democratic devices, as in Brazil and Mexico, or through powerful centralized regimes in alliance with the United States, were able to control or appease unorganized mass unrest, leaving little leeway for Communist manipulation. The problem was further complicated by the very size of the new "people weapon"; the penetration of movements affecting millions of persons, most of them unable to read or write, with few qualified

15

native leaders, was an expensive and involved undertaking which could drain the Soviet economy.

The Sino-Soviet planners therefore brought to bear a tactic lifted bodily from guerrilla warfare as it had been practiced in China by Mao, the tactic of "concentration" points, in which attacks were made, not on a broad front, but against detachments of the much stronger enemy. The principle was described in his writings by Mao several times: if the enemy has a million men with superior weapons, it would be foolhardy to launch an all-out attack against him with 200,000 men poorly equipped. However, it is quite feasible to launch an attack by a thousand men, even if their equipment is relatively inferior, against an enemy detachment of a hundred men, and score a smashing victory. Repeated over and over again, such small victories could add up to total victory. Meanwhile, as the special, concentrated actions go on, the entire enemy force can be kept in a state of agitation, off-balance, by small irritants, by the need to rush reinforcements to unexpected places, by the inability to determine what the weaker opponent was going to do next.

In the past few years, the working out of the concentration-point tactic was repeatedly shown. Wherever popular unrest seemed to be reaching an appropriate level, skilled agents, always natives of the area, penetrated the main vehicles of popular action. Except for the pioneering venture of Ho Chi Minh in Vietnam, which was an outgrowth of different circumstances, these agents at no time assumed leadership; they worked hard and efficiently for the popular movement, supported existing programs and offered tactical advice only when asked by the leaders—who soon found, how-

16

ever, that these hard-working, hard-fighting comrades knew what they were talking about and came to rely on them more and more. In fact, the assignments of these Sino-Soviet agents were specifically restricted to immediate objectives, to the building up of the organizations of the non-Communist out-group masses of people, to cultivating an awareness of the existing social set-up and its clear injustices. They initiated no talk about "communism" or "Russia" or "the new China"; in several cases they assisted out-group leaders in quieting the expostulations of local Communist parties, consisting mostly of sectarian intellectuals. Existing Communist parties, in fact, have played almost no role in any of the recent popular upheavals in the underdeveloped areas; they have, at most, and sometimes at the last minute, merely gone along with them.

The tactic was almost classically demonstrated in two cases, Laos and Cuba. In Laos, the organized out-group, the Pathet Lao, orginally had no Communists in it whatsoever, despite the availability, across the border in North Vietnam, of veteran Communist fighters. In fact, no Communist had appeared among the Pathet Lao as a leader; the nominal leader was a prince, a product of generations of aristocracy; the military leader had even expressed anti-Communist sentiments. In Cuba, the local Communist party, all during the Oriente action of Fidel Castro, stayed on more or less neutral terms with Fulgencio Batista; not a single known Communist was in the leadership circle around Castro, although anti-Castro propagandists have claimed that Ernesto Guevara, the "theoretician" of the Castro revolt, or Raul Castro, were "Communists." Guevara had some of the earmarks of an agent; but in neither case

17

was there any hard evidence of any kind of Communist party membership at any time. It is doubtful, also, in view of Sino-Soviet tactics, that any known agent would be permitted to appear so close to the top leadership.

The United States almost dramatically illustrated its inability to reply to Soviet use of the new "people base" of its foreign policy in the classic cases of Cuba and Laos. It was obvious, of course, that the United States, by use of military force on an appropriate level, could have eliminated either the Castro or the Pathet Lao movement in short order, although not without hard fighting, in view of the strong base of each among the masses of people. This action, within the existing circumstances, was made impractical for the United States for two reasons. One was that full-scale military attack would have provoked, in the case of Cuba, even greater loss of influence among the people of Latin America than was caused by the ill-fated minor attack that was tried and, in the case of Laos, not only a loss of influence in Asia but the military problem of Chinese intervention. The second and overriding reason, of course, was that such action was too dangerous, that it might have affected the delicate balance of stalemate with the Soviet Union and have led to direct conflict through some miscalculation by either side.

The United States still had no means available to counteract the Soviet Union by a corresponding use of people as a power base. In Cuba, we moved too late to set up, through a contrived *coup d'etat*, an alternative to Batista, a move which probably would not have worked anyway; we failed also in the attempt to redirect the Castro revolt through approaches to some of the men around him—in both cases using the CIA as

18

the instrument. The last-minute anti-Batista move, in effect, strengthened Castro; the approach to some of his aides merely split them off, leaving the remainder farther away from U.S. influence than before. These countermoves were not based on "people"—we had no contact and no influence among the huge Cuban outgroup; our influence, for reasons we shall explain later, was limited to the national power elite that, with the Batista dictatorship, had depended on American investments for sustenance. The more we worked with this group, the more we split it off from the majority of the people supporting Castro. (The refugee movement out of Cuba, greatly exaggerated, was limited almost entirely to this group.) In Laos we not only had no contact with the people and thus no means of arousing mass response to the Pathet Lao thrust; we had an infirm base among the tiny "power elite." The Laotian ruling group was made use of through outright purchase, with little finesse; some of its more nationalist members were offended and went with the Pathet Lao through a sense of dignity. In both cases, the Soviet Union, moving along with existing majority movements, easily outmaneuvered the United States, leaving us no recourse except, in changed circumstances, the possibility of force.

The American response to these two defeats was again typical. In the case of Cuba, it was to rush through $600 million in funds and millions more in special grants for Latin America, plus arrangement of huge amounts, from the United States and international agencies, for Brazil, correctly recognized as the eventual key to Latin American developments. In the case of Laos, it was again to hurry new, huge sums of money

19

to South Vietnam for military build-up there; to intensify our ties with the "power elite" in Thailand, already beginning to wobble in the alliance; to "beef up" the whole SEATO front; and, in an action paralleling our concentration in Latin America, on Brazil, to begin a whirlwind campaign to convert India, the key to Asian developments, into a buffer against the Sino-Soviet "people" thrust. In other words, we spread our superior forces out over a wide front, covering whole continents and subcontinents, guarding up and down the line against the next Communist move.

Obviously, at any one point along this line, where conditions of mass upheaval and power-elite weakness were ripe at any given moment, the "guerrilla" forces made use of by the Soviet Union, in line with the "concentration-point" principle, could strike and win—not with the power of arms but with the might of people—leaving the United States once more in the same quandary it faced in Laos and Cuba.

Later on we shall examine the various tactics—there is no strategy—that the United States is working out to counteract the threat of Soviet-guided upheavals, such tactics as the "Little War," tentatively rehearsed in Cuba, and shall suggest why it might be wise to reconsider the whole approach and develop our own "people power." It should be obvious meanwhile, however, that just as a military base of power can be balanced only by military means, so a "people" base of power can be balanced only by people. This is true even when the "people" power expresses itself militarily during conditions of nuclear and conventional-war stalemate.

Throughout the upheaval areas, majority protests

against continuing dominance by minority-group rulers allied with foreign investors, expressed themselves, more and more, in a special military form, with a significant strategy and ideology that gave these "risings" characteristics never before fully present in history. These were the "people weapons" the Soviet Union planned to manipulate during the nuclear stand-off to overbalance the United States.

Every year another government
seems to dissolve away, taking
our money with it.

— *Sen. Wayne Morse*

Commencement address, Suffolk
University, Boston, June 18, 1961.

3

Era of Folk War

Coincident with the development of factual military parity between the United States and the Soviet Union, a new form of "people weapon" emerged in the upheaval lands to create an unprecedented block against the secondary instruments of policy enforcement the United States had hoped to apply in those areas, to counteract Soviet thrusts. The weapon was the "folk war," a form of military and social conflict aimed by the out-group majority at the minority power elite in the underdeveloped nations and their foreign allies. While the United States was still in its nuclear dream, men who had never read Pentagon rule books fought and won wars without nuclear weapons, with-

22

out missiles and rocketry, and sometimes even without proper small arms.

The "folk wars" were not directed against the United States; but to the degree that American policy was linked to foreign-investor interests and those investors, in turn, were linked to the minority power elite in the underdeveloped lands, they became extraordinarily effective barriers to American policy enforcement; and to the same degree they became available as "people weapons" that the Soviet Union could make use of by careful maneuvering and penetration, by going with the tide, to obtain its own objectives. Because the folk war, through American default and foreign-policy flaws, became the principal weapon the Soviet Union could use against the United States during nuclear stalemate, it merits careful analysis.

Future historians may, indeed, call the middle and late twentieth century the Era of Folk War. In this new form of social and military conflict, not only nuclear weapons but conventional armament and well-trained regular troops were shown repeatedly to be of scant value. As a product, essentially, of a new condition, a nuclear and "conventional war" stalemate, folk war had key differences from the revolutionary wars of the past. It had some elements of classic revolutions—the American, French, Russian or Chinese, and even some patterns resembling those of the American Indian wars. Guerrilla tactics were a characteristic, as were the commando techniques developed principally by the British during World War II. However, there was no basis for considering the folk war to be merely a continuation of previous forms of "unconventional" conflict.

The distinguishing characteristic of the folk war

23

was not technical; rather, it was a quality related to morale and simplified ideology. The main power source was not armament—although, of course, arms were necessary in its military phase—but people, linked by a simple rationale built around obvious truths that held for each man and were clear to him out of his own life experience. Folk-war leaders went beyond this simple rationale, as will be seen in the following chapter, but the heart of folk-war theory, as distinguished from its elastic and sometimes complicated ideology or strategies, was relatively simple.

Essentially, the theory was that in a land where the satisfied ruling group, that is, those who control the wealth, is small, it follows that the dissatisfied out-group, the "have-nots," is necessarily a large majority. Therefore, if the out-group can be organized and armed it can, by force of numbers, overwhelm any individual unit of the ruling group, despite the ruling group's presumed foreign alliances and over-all superiority in armament. As unit after unit of the ruling group is vanquished, a point will be reached at which the collapse of the ruling group can be forced and the majority of the people, organized in the folk war, can sweep to victory.

Because this theory sounds too simple to be new, we should perhaps examine the previous bases of military and social conflict, to see how new it really is. International wars of the classic varieties, for example, were possible because participating nations were unified at home around a central power group and could make war as national units. Domestic unity, voluntary or enforced, was thus an essential condition in such wars; if it broke down, the war effort collapsed. The folk war, however, was possible for exactly the opposite reason: The breakdown of national unity was a prerequisite of folk war.

It should be recalled that in most of the world national unity has always been a precarious condition, more often than not imposed by force. Usually, small groups, minorities of perhaps no more than 10 per cent of the population, held the great majority in subjection. National unity of this kind was maintained, obviously, only so long as the power elite, monopolizing wealth, organization and weapons, could retain its own unity and prevent unification of the out-group majorities against it. Historically, this type of "national unity" established by a power elite has been challenged by two kinds of violent action: the *coup d'etat* and revolution. *Coups d'etat,* the traditional challenge in the underdeveloped lands of Asia, Latin America and the Moslem countries, were a means of shifting controls within the inner circle of the power elite, without majority participation. Revolutions, properly defined, were means by which one or more out-groups attempted to take control for themselves and in turn become the new power elite, with mass participation of varying depths.

Folk war traced its descent from revolution, but with a degree of mass participation rarely seen before in history. It was, moreover, a new form of revolution adapted to modern conditions of nuclear stalemate, availability of small arms, the decline of colonial empire and, particularly, the development of wide mass organization and communications. In essence, folk war was the military phase, with significant nonmilitary ramifications, of the great world-wide upheaval of the submerged peoples, the out-group majorities in the un-

25

derdeveloped or, more euphemistically, the "developing" countries. It was the military aspect of social conflict resulting from conditions in these countries, a social conflict existing in a wide belt encompassing Southeast Asia, the Middle East, North Africa, the greater part of Latin America and, in a somewhat more primitive form, the entire African continent. These lands were kept in economic subjection in varying degrees by the industrial West, particularly by what were called the colonial powers. As these powers, weakened or defeated in World War II, retrenched, the local power elite dependent on them likewise weakened. As it weakened, it was challenged by the rising out-groups, the great submerged majorities. The United States, expanding its world economic interests after World War II in the face of the tide, found itself called on inevitably to shore up the shaky and collapsing minority ruling groups, which sought to enter into symbiotic relationship with American investors as they had previously with other colonial powers of the prewar era.

To understand why the challenge of the out-group majorities most often takes a violent form, one should recall from history the fact that no group in power has ever yielded to a genuine displacing group except by force or the overwhelming threat of force. This has been true historically even in the developed countries, with their bloody record of revolution and civil war, such as those which brought about essential social change in the United States or France. In the underdeveloped areas, however, displacement of a ruling group by force is normal; there, the groups in power have no mass base; they cannot risk such safety valves as elections as a means of creating an illusion of mass participation in power, thus draining off violent reactions. Since they will not yield privilege willingly, the only way the rising majority can participate is by force.

A key point to bear in mind, one which American policy-makers with amazing frequency have failed to understand, is that folk war, as a mass action, has nothing in common with *coups d'etat*, which have no mass base and are merely factional clashes inside an existing power group. In contrast, folk war can derive its power only from the people, from the fact that it represents the aspirations of the great submerged majorities in direct antagonism to the ruling minority. Another characteristic of the folk war which American policy-makers should especially consider is that it cannot be imposed from outside. This is because a mass of people is too unwieldy for quick manipulation except in response to conditions which obviously affect the mass and are visible to the great majority of individuals composing it. Outside influences and support or opposition may, however, be important short-run factors in folk war. A developed country such as the United States or the Soviet Union can bring economic, political or military influence to bear either for or against a popular rising; and powerful developing countries, such as China or India, can also exert great influence near their own frontiers.

For those outside influences aimed at containing a folk war, however, there are problems which, in the long run, are probably insurmountable. No intervention so far has definitely altered the course of a folk war toward eventual victory; intervention has been able to hasten or postpone victory or otherwise alter schedules, but it has not changed, short of folk-war victory, the basic conditions of majority upheaval. It appears that so long as these conditions prevail, any attempt to stop a folk war, once underway, merely intensifies the eventual explosion, much as tying down a safety valve will. (This was a point to be considered by the United States in Vietnam, for example.) So far as can be judged, successful intervention in a folk war would seem to be possible only on the winning side, that is, on the side of the organized and armed majority which sooner or later, even in two generations if necessary, will overcome the minority group.

Theoretically, of course, a folk war should be preventable if an outside power could strengthen the existing power elite to a point where it would have superior force over the mass of the people, however much they may be aroused. But this possibility is defeated, first, by the numerical limit of the power elite, and second, by the impossibility of maintaining a superior force at all points and all times in the face of a determined majority. Another method, now being suggested by the United States in Latin America, is for the power elite to stave off the folk war by widening its own base and extending more privileges and economic benefits to the masses of the people; but here, too, the theory comes up against the fact that such an extension of benefits is not possible in an underdeveloped country. An extension of benefits would principally result in a reduction of benefits for the power elite; there are simply not enough to go around and still maintain the ruling group on its accustomed level. Moreover, the nature of the social system is such that any strengthening of the masses would almost surely weaken the power elite.

These inner workings of society have not been thoroughly examined by American policy-makers; in fact, Americans as a whole, bemused by word symbols which have lost their meanings, no longer understand, as their forefathers did, the artificial nature of presumed social unity. Many Americans consider their own nation and most others to be monolithic structures made up of like-thinking and like-doing individuals, except for minorities who really have only themselves to blame for being "different." This monolithic approach to social organization has blinded Americans to the nature of the world-wide upheaval of submerged peoples. A sick or starving Asian, African or Latin American is judged lazy; an energetic American in the same situation would be up and doing, studying to improve himself, working hard at his job, pushing himself up the ladder.

Societies in general, however, are something like pyramids. The occasional brilliant or ruthless individual can shove himself to the top; but when he does so in a fixed society, such as those in the upheaval areas, he must at each step of the way displace someone else in a well-established position. The pyramidal structure remains intact; the great mass remains on the bottom regardless of the freak rise or fall of the individual.

A factor in the American failure to understand the more typical world beyond our borders has been that American society, until recently at least, has allowed more leeway; the frontiers of geography and technology could expand, providing room for an ever larger pyramid and more movement up or down. All modern governments, however, including the American, have resulted from revolutions, directly or indirectly, distantly or immediately. They have resulted from a mass movement upward to displace the group at the top of the pyramid. In all cases, the power to be on top was originally taken by force from one group by another. In some cases, after taking power, the new group broadened its base slowly or rapidly; in others, power was kept jealously within narrow limits.

The United States itself is an example of a government, originally produced by revolution, which, through Jeffersonian influence, broadened its power base; Spain exemplifies a power group which functions within extremely narrow limits of power, with huge out-group masses. In general, those governments which broadened the power base became democracies, as usually defined; those which did not remained dictatorships. It should be noted, however, that the member of the out-group, the non-participant in power, has little more to say about his government in a democracy than he does in a dictatorship; he is equally subject to the concealed or overt iron hand whenever he strays from the broad or narrow path delineated for him. The difference is that in the underdeveloped areas of folk war, where the power base is narrow and jealously limited, the out-group necessarily becomes the vast majority, the genuine nation, and not a "different" minority as in the United States. In the upheaval lands the "different" minority is in fact the power elite.

An additional factor, possibly shocking to the American mind, is that all law, except for various formalisms derived from habit, is specifically aimed at restraining the out-groups and protecting the interests of the power group, however broad or narrow its bases. Although this fact is patent to any member of the vast out-group majorities in the upheaval lands of present or future folk war, the citizen of a Western democracy is shielded from it, because the broader the base of power, the fewer will be the out-group members; thus, in his society, with a broad power base, laws will be widely acceptable, in fact beneficial as a rule, for the majority. Also, in more developed societies, various illusions of power-sharing, such as elections to determine nonbasic issues, are cultivated to enhance acceptance of laws. In the upheaval lands, the luxury of such illusions cannot be permitted; any uncontrolled mass vote, for example, would be out of the question—the false nature of any permitted issue would be too evident. Who could imagine, in mid-1961 conditions, a free election in Spain, Portugal, Paraguay, Vietnam, Korea, Taiwan, Iran or Saudi Arabia? For this reason, in fact, folk-war leaders, before or after victory, normally ignore elections; they often consider them to be nonbasic even in countries as advanced as the United States.

American understanding of the nature of the folk war is also hindered by the fact that in our society, the menace of the out-groups, except possibly for the Negro minority in a few Southern states, is practically non-existent. In well-organized societies like our own, the necessities of life are in sufficient quantity to enable most people to live above the subsistence level. In such societies, danger will arise only after organizational breakdown, as might be brought on by defeat in war or prolonged economic catastrophe—conditions which in effect create majority out-groups where none were before, as in Germany after World War I. In the poorly organized societies characteristic of the underdeveloped countries of Asia, Africa and Latin America, areas of potential or actual folk war, circumstances are different

31

indeed. There, production facilities provide no more than mere subsistence on an insecure level for most people; therefore the minority group in power, even if well-intentioned, is obliged to maintain control with an iron hand. The base of power, because of the scarcity of consumables, particularly valued items, must be kept as narrow as possible; even social elements which, because of economic aspirations, would tend to be natural allies of the power elite are carefully excluded.

In the past, before the era of folk war, poor national organization saved these minority rulers from revolution; they remained as small islands of organized force in a sea of amorphous and undirected hostility. The threats that arose came, rather, from their own fringes, which now and then would try to move in with them to share the power and the benefits. The fringe groups, as they were rebuffed, often attempted to force their way in, striking at the power center in *coups d'etat* or "banana revolts." If successful, however, the *coup d'etat* merely transferred power from one small group to another, in no way altering the basic power pattern; the vast out-group majorities remained untouched and usually uninterested. The great majority was unorganized, separated, each individual scrabbling to survive and aware that there was nothing at all that he could do to improve his lot, by himself.

The amazing change that took place in the underdeveloped countries, to lead to the present period of upheaval and folk war, will be described more in context in Chapter 10, but it should be summarized here. It was modern industrial capital, entering the area in symbiotic alliance with the local power elite, which sowed the seeds of change. To ensure profits, capital necessarily had to introduce economic organization of the people, which in turn led to social organization. For the first time in history, the majorities became aware of themselves. This process can be seen even by the casual observer in any underdeveloped country where American investment has penetrated, even in less developed parts of our own country, as when factories draw labor from the North Carolina hills as raw individualists and find them shortly joining trade unions. Against the new organization of the out-groups, however, the power elite could balance its alliance with the foreign investors; and, in need, it could tap the might of the investors' homeland to retain its position, even calling on tanks, planes or napalm. For the out-groups to overcome this alliance, even with all the might of their new organization, much more than a simple revolution was necessary.

Thus the theory of folk war grew out of the requirements of the new power alignment, out of the need to produce a means of overcoming the alliance between the local power elite and foreign investment capital. The threat of the out-groups, of course, intensified the dependency of the power elite on its foreign ally; and it thus lost its national character to become the equivalent of the "Tories" in the American Revolution. For this reason folk wars have taken on a patriotic character—of wars against "the foreign devil" and his native "lackeys"; the combination of patriotism and economic motivation creates an irresistible morale. When the majorities add arms to their organization, and when to the arms they add the theory of folk war, of whittling down the enemy, they can no longer be contained. The foreign investors will tend to support their native subsidiary with more and more arms and money only for

33

a limited period, short or long; at some point, the probability of return on the investment diminishes to the vanishing point. When this happens the foreign investor group (and their home country) lose motivation; they abandon their native allies. The folk war thereupon sweeps to victory.

Many of America's foreign-policy defeats in the underdeveloped areas of the world, if examined coldly and without preconceptions, will be seen to be byproducts of just such victories by the folk war, not all of them assisted by the Soviet Union. There will be more such defeats for our foreign policy, so long as it is linked through our investors to declining minority groups; the "folk warriors" are growing more and more sure. Initial victories have given them confidence, not only in majority power, but in the ideology that guides many of them. Let us take a look at that ideology.

> ... this struggle which we call ideological, but which is really the age-old struggle of humanity.
>
> — Editorial, New York *Herald-Tribune*

4

Ideology of Upheaval

"In the beginning was the Word" (John 1:1); and the word, in the sense of a moving ideology, a method of analysis and action, has become an increasingly common characteristic of modern upheavals, particularly in the unique folk-war form. The common ideology, as it has penetrated in the underdeveloped areas where lately organized majority out-groups are challenging age-old minority rule, has obvious roots in Marxism. Its practitioners and expounders, however, are not Communists and often clash with local Communist groups even when allied with them against the power elite. Marxism, to be sure, is a word symbol which frightens many grown Americans, including our policy-shapers;

35

so, as a semantic aid to understanding, one should perhaps call this new, simplified and heretic version by another name. A name with good Greek roots, by scientific custom, should do; we may call it, say "Diaclanism" (*diaklan:* "break through" against an opposite).

In wide areas of Africa, Asia, and Latin America, where even the dream of a comfortable living is limited to possibly 10 per cent of the population, the basic Marxist thesis of change through the clash of opposite forces, which Karl Marx took from a ponderous Teutonic philosopher named George Wilhelm Friedrich Hegel who in turn adapted it from the ancient Greeks, seems both logical and obvious. The clash is right there before their eyes—the poverty-stricken, diseased and exploited 90 per cent versus the overfed 10 per cent of the ruling clique. To the ideologists of this new "diaclanism," the necessity of force to bring about change is also obvious; in an economy producing barely enough for them, the ruling 10 per cent certainly could not be expected to give up their privileges willingly. Diaclanism also frequently inveighs against the profit system; the idea of not making profits off other people's work is easy for the majority group to accept—they have never made a profit anyway.

As for the eventual utopia of communism, however, which the Russian or Chinese "pure" Marxists insist on, the masses of people in the upheaval areas do not seem, so far, to be much impressed; it is too far in the future and they want to eat now. Only in areas where Communists, after a period of alliance with the popular movement, have taken it over—usually because of Western attacks on the majority movement—has the strait way to communism been taken. To form their simplified diaclanistic ideology, the upheaval leaders have abstracted the "common sense" aspects of Marxism, stripped it of futuristic or immediately nonessential qualities, then adapted what was left to their immediate conditions of struggle. Men such as Sukarno of Indonesia, Nehru of India, Nkrumah of Ghana, Touré of Guinea, Castro of Cuba, even Nasser of Egypt or Prince Souvanna Phouma of Laos are, in this sense, diaclanists. Mao Tsetung, of course, Ho Chi Minh and, to a degree, Josef Broz Tito remain as "pure" Marxists, who continue to debate "Marxism" with Soviet ideologists; the diaclanists, however, are uninterested in hair-splitting. So far as can be judged, all popular leaders in the upheaval areas, except for those tied economically to the foreign-investor groups, have tinges of diaclanism, which, as an ideology, may have become even more irritating to the Soviet Union and China than it is, for other reasons, to most Westerners. In fact, the reaction of most Westerners to any ideology is not unlike that of the late H. Goering to intellectualism, that is, to reach for a gun. The reason is probably the same in both cases, a cultivated inability to understand, a fault which ended unhappily for Goering, and could produce similar unhappiness for Westerners.

The permeating effect of diaclanism is, however, clearly evident in its role as a guiding ideology in the folk war, the disciplined majority upheaval against minority power centers allied with foreign investors. It has tended to be less important or at least less apparent in the economic field, as opposed to the military aspects of social change, in most of the upheaval lands, which may be because economics is considerably more complicated even than warfare. But it is as an ideology of analysis of social forces, as a guide to political and military action, that diaclanism is of interest to the West.

The accumulating political and military successes of popular movements in the upheaval lands have taken place often in the face of apparently impossible odds. To most of the West, they came as complete surprises. That was one reason, apart from America's immersion in fantasy, why these successes were explained away as due to "luck," or "circumstances," or "America's failure to act," or, in the terms of a past decade, "treason in high places." One might consider the possibility that the successes resulted from the fact that the upheaval leaders knew what they were doing while their opponents did not. That these leaders all to some degree used diaclanism as their system of analysis, indicates that the system might deserve examination.

Molecular movements obey general laws, although the actions of individual particles may not always be predictable. It is conceivable, therefore, that social organizations set up by man may also obey general laws, though the individual may not be predictable. Wars and other forms of conflict, as a manifestation of man's social organization at this stage of his development, might also have determinable laws.

Diaclanist leaders of upheaval in the underdeveloped areas have assumed that these laws are knowable and that man can act in accordance with his knowledge of them. They examine the "play of forces," adding a little weight here, taking away a little there—a philosophical ju-jitsu—until the whole balance slides in the desired direction. It is their system of analysis, they believe, which permits them to determine the forces and where and when to apply or remove pressure to bring about desired results.

The system presumes that change begins inside society, because of inner conflicts. Outside forces have an effect, but it is mechanical, concerning changes in size or amount, or, to some extent, timing; their effect on qualities, on intrinsic conflicts, is relatively minor. Outside forces, the theory goes, affect the conditions of change; but it is the inner forces of society which are the basis of change. An example of this interpretation often used by the popular leaders in argument is that of a duck and an egg: The duck sits on an egg as an "outside force" and eventually hatches a duckling—but she could sit on a doorknob forever and there would be no duckling, because the inside factors are different.

In this analysis, contradictory inner forces are thoroughly studied, then ways of intensifying or resolving the contradictions are developed and tested. Contradictory forces, opposite drives, are looked for in every process, because it is believed that the interplay of these drives and the clash between them will decide the result. All social movement, backward or forward, results from this interplay of contradictory drives. The simplified examples given are plus and minus, action and reaction, positive and negative, fusion and splitting, advance and withdrawal, "haves" and "have-nots," and so on. Thought itself is believed to be a product of contradictory ideas that finally come together to solve a problem.

In theory, during this analysis, great care is taken to avoid looking at a new problem with a preformed opinion or to look at only part of it rather than its whole aspect. Changes in relationships and qualities that occur as a particular social process develops are also studiously observed. Each developmental step, it is believed, produces a qualitative change that must be taken into account. The basic contradictions or opposite drives remain, however, and tend to intensify as the opposite drives take on new qualities, although allowance is made for the possibility of "reverse movement." The key objective of the analysis, as it refers to conditions of folk war or pre-upheaval, is to find and understand the main contradiction, that of the two principal drives that are meeting head-on, and discover how to resolve it in favor of the rising majority out-group and against the minority "power elite."

This analysis has led to rather significant developments. Although, quite clearly, the basic "contradiction" in the underdeveloped lands has historically been the fight, open or hidden, between the ruling minority and the great majority of the people, diaclanists and similar analysts have at certain stages been able to produce a temporary "resolution" of this contradiction, in great part, to turn a united nation against a foreign investor group for a short period. This happened in Mexico, as early as the "oil war" of the 1930's, mostly fought with propaganda weapons; during the initial phase of the Castro rising in Cuba; and during the Anglo-French attack on Suez. Attempts to do this failed in two cases during the early 1950's, the CIA-sponsored *coups d'etat* in Iran and Guatemala, because the "popular movement" really had no majority base and the fight against the *coup d'etat* could not be turned into a folk war. After the temporary unity of the contradictory forces of "minority" and "majority" has achieved its objective, the opposite drives again tend to come to the fore. In Cuba, the folk-war drive came out of the temporary alliance on top; and the former ruling minority was eliminated, pending outside aid. In Egypt, a wing of the ruling minority came out essentially on top in a preliminary upheaval, but greatly increased its mass base, to alter conditions. In Mexico, a pioneer folk-war area, the leaders of the out-group majority came to the top, but in conditions of poor popular organization they found themselves obliged to adopt the role, to a considerable extent, of the previous ruling minority—although with significant "qualitative" changes. In Iran and Guatemala, the capping of the "popular movement" tended to stimulate organization of the out-group, with conditions of explosion developing that folk-war leaders prepared to take advantage of.

New developments have led to some recent revisions in the analytical trend of diaclanism by popular leaders in the upheaval areas. There is among them now a tendency to define the basic contradictions in their areas, the opposite drives, in terms of "nation" versus "imperialism," that is, the whole people against foreign-investor groups. The importance of the local power elite is seen as minor, whether it goes with or against "imperialism," and, in practice, it is considered an ally of the foreign-investor group rather than the rising national majority, to be won over if possible, to be destroyed if not. This appears to be a result of analysis of conditions produced by concentrations of power, both economic and military, in the hands of the United States and the ability of American foreign investors to call on this power as needed. Thus the key enemy becomes American power, not the local power-clique, and the key contradiction is found in the weight of Ameri-

41

can arms and money versus the weight of the folk-war masses of people.

Although the diaclanists of the upheaval areas, following their analytical system, look for the two principal contradictory forces in social development, they do not expect to find two equal forces. They believe that growth is uneven and that if two opposite drives become equal, the equality will be only momentary. At any given time, they hold, one drive will in some degree be stronger than the other. They watch carefully, therefore, to determine when the force they support achieves strength enough to overbalance its opposite, or when the force they oppose becomes so strong that a temporary retreat is in order.

Unlike revolutionary chieftains of the past, the folk-war leaders believe in patience, a quality they have perhaps inherited from centuries of poverty where endurance was a prime requisite to survival, but which also comes from their adherence to diaclanism. They assume that the more a force builds up, the deeper its inner contradiction and the greater its tendency to fly apart. Many are convinced that the great American build-up of overseas power, aimed at the folk war, will produce tremendous inner contradictions in American society—economic dislocations, social maladjustments, lopsided growth of war industries—and eventually, a dictatorial effort to resolve the contradictions by force. As the inner contradictions grow, changes of a qualitative nature will occur until, in a sudden burst, American power will fall apart. Not all the folk-war leaders hold this view; in fact, the "pure Marxists" among them follow Mao Tse-tung, who appeared to think that

American power would have to be taken apart—at some future "correct time," of course.

Among the diaclanists, none of whom, of course, is a Communist—if he were, he would be purged as a heretic—there is a belief that time is on their side almost as a matter of fate, so far as eventual elimination of the "opposite drive" of American power is concerned. It will retreat, they believe, and then the folk wars will sweep to victory around the underdeveloped areas of the world, easily overwhelming the isolated islands of the local power elite left helpless as American-investor support is withdrawn.

Since most diaclanists, as individual leaders, have had their conflicts with local Communists, they are not looking forward too eagerly to a time when the main balance of forces, the main "contradictions," may be between the folk-war nations and the Communist world, an eventual "contradiction" which they are led to directly in the extrapolation of events in line with their system of analysis. In their lifetimes they have seen how the main "opposite drives" have changed in the upheaval areas from "out-group majority versus minority power elite," to "out-group majority versus alliance of the minority elite with foreign investors," and now, as they think, to "folk war versus American power." The next stage, they fear, may be "folk war versus Communist power." When that time comes, so their extrapolation goes, the Soviet Union and China, instead of moving with them in alliance, will attempt openly to take over the tide of upheaval and channel it directly toward the Communist goal. They point to examples of this development in folk-war areas, such as North Vietnam, where the relative weakness of American

43

power eliminated it as a key factor and left the field to the "contradictory forces" of "folk war versus Communist power"—with rapid absorption of the folk-war forces by the Communists glossing over the "resolution of the contradiction." All of Southeast Asia, it is felt, is rapidly moving into this phase of development; the growth of regional Russo-Chinese power, relative to American, may eliminate American power as the main "opposite drive" in the area.

There should be considerable room for thought provided, for American global strategists, in this extrapolation. By their own ideology, the diaclanists will, at some period determined by analysis of the relative strength of the contradictory forces involved, tend to cultivate American power to balance Sino-Soviet power and enable their own movement to come through, regionally, on top of both; just as now, as a result of their analyses of relative strength, the diaclanists tend to cultivate Soviet power. It is interesting to note that the tactic of balancing off opposite powers to obtain independent maneuverability is being used to a degree by non-Marxist and even anti-Marxist leaders—such as Jânio Quadros, president of Brazil, key country of Latin America, who has gestured toward the Soviet Union and the neutralist nations, not merely to get relatively string-free loans from the United States as an American countermeasure (which he obtained), but mainly to provide a balance within which he could carry out his own nationalist plan for building Brazil in line with its own needs.

However, there are two sides to the coin. It would seem that the United States, if it can set its policies in line with national interest, could by careful maneuver-

ing choose allies at just those points in the underdeveloped areas where, from the standpoint of global
strategy, they might be most useful: that is, among the
developing nations whose leaders, threatened by growing Soviet power, before or after folk-war success, seek
to balance it with American power to prevent Communist take-over.

If the analysis is correct—it could be, considering
previous diaclanist accuracy—then the stronger the
Sino-Soviet power becomes after the critical point in
each area of upheaval, the more the nationalist upheaval leaders might consider an effective alliance with
the United States to balance it off. This would be a perspective indeed: the United States for the first time
since the golden days of World War II identified with
the majority movements in the underdeveloped areas.
Moreover, despite Sino-Soviet concentration, the alliance of American power with the folk war, instead of
against it, could undoubtedly overbalance the Sino-
Soviet drive much as, in reverse, the present American
drive against the folk wars has been overbalanced on
a contrary basis.

The possibility would remain wild speculation, of
course, so long as American power could not free itself
from private interest and take the side of the folk war,
or American policy-makers remained unable to abandon their "red" or "white" preconceptions. It indicates,
however, a rich new field for exploration by Americans who feel it is time to look for a rational foreign
policy and to look newly, considering all opportunities
to win instead of lose. A short course in "diaclanism," or
straight Marxism, for that matter—regardless of scien-

tific accuracies or inaccuracies—might also prove helpful for American foreign affairs experts.

Even the devil can quote scripture without following its precepts; Americans, presumably on God's side, should be strong enough to resist contamination by any false doctrine they might encounter. So far, however, even after the folk war has won and preserved itself from Soviet power, and its leaders have sought friendly intercourse with us—as in the case of Indonesia—we have held them at arm's length, called them "anti-American" and, by continuous "contrary" maneuvers, driven them ever more deeply into "neutralism" at best and to pro-Soviet policies at worst. Let us take a brief look at our problem in a clear-cut case, Indonesia, as a footnote to these two chapters on folk war.

A FOLK-WAR FOOTNOTE: INDONESIA

As the war in the Far East ended in 1945, the people of the Netherlands East Indies were winning a folk war of their own, spurring the retreat of the Japanese invaders who had taken over the sprawling series of giant and tiny islands from the Dutch, nipping their heels in guerrilla operations by small bands that caused more Japanese casualties than had all Allied attacks in the area. As the Japanese fled, the people declared independence and established the Republic of Indonesia to become the fifth most populous nation in the world and the largest Moslem country. When the Dutch, aided by U.S.-trained marines and U.S. arms, attempted to retake Indonesia, the folk war met them head-on. In four years of savage attack and counterattack, the Dutch,

46

too, were defeated and were obliged to recognize
Indonesian independence in 1949.

The Indonesian folk war was won; and at that
point came the crisis which appears now to be typical
of folk wars. The winning majority, ousting the Dutch
and confiscating their properties and those of their
domestic "Tory" allies, encountered a characteristic
difference in its own ranks. The majority split into
groups following pro-Communist leaders opposed by
much greater numbers who continued with the purely
national goals that had given direction to the folk
war. A bloody civil war ensued; the national majority
smashed the Communist opposition and took full charge
of the new Republic. Within five years the government
of Indonesia, working with a people 95 per cent illiterate after 300 years of Dutch rule, had taught 35 million
to read and write; the words of Jefferson and Lincoln
were circulated throughout the land; the Indonesians
turned hopefully to the United States, the origin of
these wonderful "new" ideas, for support in consolidat-
ing their republic. They received none.

The stumbling-block did not directly concern the
link between United States investors and the Dutch;
American holdings, except for oil interests and the new
speculative capital that had entered after Dutch de-
parture, were small. But the United States, as the 1950's
dawned, was immersed, it will be recalled, in panic;
the word symbol "communism" was drowning out reason. United States refusal of meaningful assistance to
the new Indonesia grew out of "fear" that the republic,
which had just put down its native Communists in
blood, would not resist "communism" in its march
from China and Vietnam down through Indonesia to

Australia. The United States therefore supported the Dutch, our NATO allies, in their continued occupation of the Indonesian territory of West Irian (Dutch New Guinea), which had been part of the East Indies administrative complex for a century, considering it, in the peculiar "geographic" strategy fashionable at the time, to be a barrier against southward Communist expansion.

If, after our Revolution, our "proto-folk war," the British had retained by force the territories west of the Appalachians, would Americans have yielded gracefully? How would we have viewed a foreign power, stronger even than the British, which helped them in holding our territories? The Indonesian reaction was exactly what our foreign policy experts could have predicted if they had been familiar with America's colonial past and our Revolution; but in the panic period we were being guided mainly by ideological casualties of Europe and by unassimilated elements attempting to be *Americani Americanorum,* who knew nothing of our past. Indonesians who attempted to talk to these supposedly American "policy-makers" complained that "the Americans have never heard of Jefferson." The disillusion was sharp; it was reflected not only abroad but at home. In its foreign policy, the new Indonesian Republic switched from early pro-Americanism to outright "independence"; and was immediately condemned by John Foster Dulles who at that time was grouping "neutralists" with the Soviet Union and proclaiming that those who were not with us were against us.

In its domestic policy, Indonesia abandoned its approach to Jeffersonian democracy and took the road, soon to become typical of folk wars, toward "guided democracy," in which emergency powers were vested in President Sukarno, a folk-war hero. It accepted assistance from the Soviet Union; it took proffered aid from the Colombo Plan; and when the United States, slowly awakening, finally offered help on an extremely modest scale, Indonesia accepted it only with careful national controls. In the place of an eager friend, we now had a reserved and cautious neutral.

Strangely enough, even after the panic declined somewhat in the United States, permitting a hint of reason to re-enter foreign affairs, the American attitude toward Indonesia was very little revised. When President Sukarno came to Washington, he was received coolly and formally; *The New York Times,* whose earlier anti-Indonesian editorials by the late Robert Aura Smith had aroused official Indonesian protests, commented unfavorably on Indonesia's claim to her territory of West Irian, no longer from pro-Dutch sentiment but perhaps from habit, or from routine perusal of "morgue" clips of Smith's editorials. To Americans, Indonesia was unimportant and unheard of: a country of 90 million people, a key Moslem nation lying in a strategic world area, exposed to the "people power" manipulations of the Soviet Union, was blindly ignored. But when Sukarno went to Moscow, Khrushchev laid down red carpets for his every step; he wined and dined him, danced the "Indonesia Free" cha-cha-cha with him (according to newspaper reports); offered him loans, services, technicians—anything he might want. When Sukarno went to Peking, the Chinese rulers attempted to outdo Khrushchev; they rushed him through tours of the newest and best installations suitable also for Indonesia; they proclaimed eternal friendship; pushed aside as unimportant Sukarno's expulsion of nearly a million Chinese from his country; hurriedly agreed to all he asked.

A major lesson which can be learned from folk war in Southeast Asia is that colonial actions and attitudes, whether direct, as undertaken there by the Dutch or the French, or more or less "indirect," as undertaken there by the United States, are open invitations to Communist penetration. Where this penetration has been successful, as in North Vietnam, rural South Vietnam, and now to a growing degree in Laos, it has been carried out principally on the basis of nationalist and anti-colonial slogans, interspersed with the age-old cries for land and bread. Obviously, continued Dutch occupation of Indonesian territory cannot be accepted by the Republic of Indonesia; sooner or later a clash will occur; and at that time, what will happen? The events, without the aid of soothsayer equipment, are not hard to extrapolate. The Soviet Union, China, the entire Afro-Asian bloc, much of Latin America, the new African nations, will all side with Indonesia; the United States, caught in its "geographic" analysis of "Communist" penetration, will side with the Dutch, deserted by all but the English-speaking Commonwealth, the Western European powers and a few dependent dictatorships such as Spain and Portugal—the precise line-up which even rudimentary knowledge of foreign policy requirements at this stage would lead any American policy-maker to avoid under all circumstances.

Indonesia could instead become a test case for a new, corrected American approach to the problem of the folk war and its aftereffects on the contest between the United States and the Soviet Union. It would seem that both long-range strategy and immediate tactics in this conflict—quite apart from our adherence or non-adherence to our own Jeffersonian principles—would oblige the United States to move speedily to correct its policies toward folk war areas generally and toward Indonesia in particular; to support Indonesia's case against the Dutch and its claims against Dutch-occupied territories, in the United Nations, if necessary, and by friendly pressure on the Dutch outside the United Nations, preferably; to quiet Australia's fears, originally caused by us, that Indonesian occupation of West Irian might open "a highway" for "Communist attack, doing so possibly through an agreement between Australia and Indonesia for joint defense of the area, with our help, in the event of the hypothetical attack; and, above all, to "warm up" to the sensitive and intelligent Indonesians themselves, cultivating them as equals, still eager to learn from our own post-colonial experiences, if we will only let them.

The sum total of innumerable relative truths may be the absolute truth.

— *Mao Tse-tung*

5

The Reddening Tide

Principally because of the blind help it received from erroneous American foreign policy, the Soviet Union was able to move with the tide of popular upheaval in the underdeveloped areas and to manipulate it, here and there, at strategic points, to increase its effectiveness as a weapon against American policy. Instead of countering this Soviet maneuver, American policy-makers planned attacks against the folk war itself such as the "Little War" (discussed in Chapter 9). Yet it should have been clear that the folk war in itself was by no means Communist or even Communist-dominated, as we have seen in the discussion so far, although it may still become so if American policy persists in its present direction.

The decision to mark off the folk war as Communist would not seem to have been wholly a product of interested propaganda or of "intelligence" reports received from CIA agents closely linked with endangered minority cliques in the upheaval lands, a factor we shall discuss in chapter 7. The decision may, in fact, have been produced in part by a peculiar American blind spot that has influenced many of our reactions in recent years, an irrational fear of the very thought of "communism," which has become a strange word symbol, one of many which now tend to govern American actions. The very nature of social upheaval, crystal clear to Americans of Jefferson's day, has been almost entirely obscured in the minds of Americans—people and leaders, since the emergence of the Soviet Union as a world power.

Man's natural tendency, cultivated to enable him to get on with his job and avoid debate over details, is to think and judge in black and white, disregarding gradations. Americans for the most part, in viewing social change, now have a similar tendency to think and judge in *red* and white, disregarding a whole spectrum of other shades and colors. This arbitrary and naïve approach is of course a direct result of the fear engendered by the power conflict between the United States and the Soviet Union. In this conflict, we have felt, the nations and peoples of the world must either be for us or against us; they are either red or white.

Even the average American dare not, in these times of crisis, allow himself such simplified thinking; indulged in by policy-makers and opinion-shapers it becomes highly dangerous, for in this age of specialization they have taken on a responsibility to decide for the nation as a whole. The simplification is dangerous, not merely because it is illogical or in error, but because, in foreign policy, it tends to isolate the United States and strengthen the hand of the Soviet Union.

Once the emotional blind spot is overcome, it should be rather easy for most Americans, product of the first colonial revolution, to understand that the rising tide of the submerged peoples is no more a creation of communism than are the tides of the sea. A hungry man does not need either a Communist or a Capitalist to tell him he must eat. A landless farmer does not require the assistance of a Soviet agent to discover that he wants land. A slave does not dream of freedom because someone tells him to. An American, of all people on earth, should know these things intuitively. The strivings of the submerged peoples are instinctively directed toward improving their lot by all available means, including force; this fact is as old as man. The folk war is merely a modern form the force for change is taking, a form produced by the conditions of our era in the underdeveloped lands.

When folk-war struggle begins, if it seems significant enough or politically or geographically of interest, it is then that the Soviet Union steps in with offers of help to the rising majority. If the battle is hard, which it normally is, the folk-war leaders reasonably and eagerly accept the proffered assistance. They observe that other foreigners, the investors, have already sided with their enemies, the minority power elite; Soviet assistance provides a needed and available balance. The United States, urged by its investors, then moves to protect

54

them and to counter the Soviet Union's assistance to the folk war. At this point, if not before, the folk war is presented to the people of the United States, by the public relations experts of the investors and the "information" or "intelligence" specialists of the government, as "a new Red attack against a freedom-loving ally of the West." This of course is nonsense; the rise of a majority in an attempt to control their own county is neither red nor white in origin; it is the normal, natural and Jeffersonian drive of the dissatisfied toward satisfaction, of the have-nots toward having.

The name, however, will often lead to the game; both the United States and the Soviet Union tend to believe their own propaganda. The leaders of the rebelling majorities become "Red Heroes" to the Soviet Union and "Red agents" to the United States. The United States tends to go overboard deeper even than the Soviet Union in this respect. Nasser of Egypt, after accepting Soviet aid, was called a Red agent in the United States at the same time that he was imprisoning and torturing native Egyptian Communists. The Soviet Union, of course, welcomes the American procedure. It is naturally pleased when American investors, for reasons analyzed in Chapter 10, become frightened for the safety of the minority clique they are bound to in alliance and on whom, they presume, their profits depend, and call on American power to protect the status quo. The United States, in responding, is of course placed squarely on the side that sooner or later will lose. At the same time the Soviet Union, simply by following its national interests, is able to play the role of protector of the embattled majority and to dramatize by every propaganda device its alliance with the folk war.

Because it can align its own strategic interests with the popular movements, the Soviet Union is able to penetrate and influence them in varying degrees, although the folk-war majority is seeking not "Communism," but the democratic right to control its own destinies. In view of American foreign policy and our negative official attitude toward the folk war, however, the wonder is not that the Soviet Union has been able in many instances to penetrate the popular upheaval movements, but that it has not already turned the whole massive tide of the world's submerged peoples against the United States.

It should be clear by now that in the folk war the cards were not stacked in favor of the Soviet Union through some mysterious and cunning sleight-of-hand by Khrushchev. They were stacked against the United States *by the United States.* Yielding to the importunities of its overseas investors, even accepting as true their necessarily one-sided interpretations of local developments, the United States has adopted policies largely in their private interest, not necessarily in the national interests of the people of the United States. These policies have led directly to defeat at each point of test. The defeats are mounting up to a dangerous degree; and we shall therefore study the causes and possible cures of this policy flaw at some length in Part III.

It is also possible that ideological confusion on the official level has led United States policy-makers to consider the folk-war tide as red. Actually, a simplified, heretical form of Marxism, which we have called "diaclanism," is the ideological guide for most of the folk-war leaders. An indication that it has been confused with communism can be found in our intelligence reports and even in official American statements labeling many popular leaders as "Communists," as in the case of Africa's Nkrumah or Touré, or even Indonesia's Sukarno, who, as noted, defeated his local Communists in a bloody civil war that followed folk war victory over the Dutch and the Indonesian "Tories." Continual mistaken evaluations of this kind have even produced opposite reactions among American policy-makers, who, fearing still another wrong guess, on occasion have considered genuine Communists to be mere agrarian reformers.

A sincere attempt by American policy-makers, on the basis of unbiased data, to examine the composition of each social movement in the underdeveloped countries and discover its true objectives and the methods its leaders use to reach them, could shape policy decisions in each area that would be in our best national interest. It is true that in the folk-war period the great out-group majorities tend to gather around immediate goals, uniting different inner tendencies; but within this over-all nationalist grouping, which fights together against the common enemy, the ruling minority clique, there are seeds of future development with colorations ranging through the political spectrum, from primitive anarchism to totalitarianism.

Within this spectrum, in varying degrees of weakness or strength, one normally finds the two basically contradictory trends: the one based on faith in people, faith in the majority, which we may call Jeffersonian in principle; and the one based on faith in the Russian or Chinese examples, which we may call communistic, for lack of a better description. The Soviet Union, with its Chinese ally, manipulates the tendency which favors it; the United States most often blindly fights against its own natural allies among the rising majorities, forcing them into neutralist or even pro-Soviet positions, as we have shown. Even when the folk war wins and the proto-Jeffersonian nationalist trend maintains control against communistic power seekers, the United States has tended to back the "counterrevolution" of the defeated minority clique or permitted its overseas business interests to do so, thus once more forcing the nationalists into pro-Soviet gestures to balance American enmity.

American liberals and American conservatives have sinned equally in this respect. The conservative, in red-and-white insistence that all foreigners be 100 per cent American although they have non-American problems to solve, the liberal, in also insisting that even in a period of revolution the foreign nation set up an American two-party system—though even the United States did not do so—have been "gold-dust" twins demonstrating provincial ignorance in parallel terms. There has never been a revolution which permitted freedom for the enemies of the revolution; and we may assume that the folk wars, the most basically revolutionary of all conflicts, will be "undemocratic" in that sense. Probably the most we can expect of the new nationalism, for the present, is the "guided democracy" espoused by a whole range of nationalist leaders from Touré to Sukarno. However, the less the new nationalists have to fear from manipulations by the Soviet Union or the United States, the quicker they can move toward representative democracy. Our policy-makers have to decide whether or not we are in favor in fact of what we claim to favor in theory.

Meanwhile, American policy toward the tide of social upheaval has been a compound of confusion, ignorance and one-sided private interests, in which the over-all national interests of the United States have not been considered. The result has been to strengthen the influence of the Soviet Union in the folk-war areas and throughout the developing lands far more than it could have done itself. We may conclude, therefore, that the rising tide of the folk war, while neither red nor white in origin, is tending to redden (through American default) and that it may redden all the more if the United States continues what amounts to all-out assistance to the Soviet Union. In dyeing the tide with red, the United States has been the Soviet Union's best possible ally.

Let us pass on to Part II, to see how the same basic flaw has blunted the instruments of American policy formation and enforcement on a wide front.

PART 2

INSTRUMENTS OF POLICY

Remembering our own history, it is easier for us to sympathize with the new nations.

— Adlai Stevenson

6

Against the World Turning

American awakening to the new world alignment of forces and balances was slow and incomplete. Accompanying the new administration to Washington in the crisis year of 1961 was a group of "adjusted liberals" of the so-called Harvard set, who, despite years of cultivation of "double-think" in their public writings and pronouncements, nevertheless retained as a heritage from their Roosevelt-era mentors a vestigial skill in analysis. They could see the problem; but their years of adjustment inhibited them in presentation of answers. Through their cautious but essentially correct definition of the problem, however, United States policy-makers for the first time became aware that somehow the previous bases of American and Soviet power had been balanced off, and that a new base, a new leverage—people, had become, within the shaky conditions of stalemate, the key instrument of policy enforcement—and of American defeat.

Unfortunately, the adjusted liberals did not dare follow through, in their analysis, to the obvious sequitur. It was clear that if people—specifically, the majority out-groups in the upheaval lands—had become the new leverage of power, then it had also become a matter of life or death for the United States either to assume control of that leverage or to neutralize it. The Harvard set, however, had long ago barked their shins in a modest tea-room conflict with American business interests; and they were by no means eager to give up their newly regained status in a similar engagement. No attempt was made, therefore, to point out that the only way the United States could stop the increasingly successful Soviet attempt to take over the new people power and direct it against the United States, was to go with the upheaval tide and not try to stem it or roll it back.

There were some minor suggestions that the United States reduce its support for the corrupt dictatorships that had gathered under the wing of the American eagle; but these suggestions were correctly rejected. Unless America moved to the side of the majorities as well, mere reduction of such support in the face of a hostile popular movement would have been an open invitation to the Soviet Union. Moreover, American withdrawal of support and the consequent assumption of power by the national majorities we had opposed would have endangered the military bases so painstakingly erected around the perimeter of the Soviet Union.

64

Even more to the point, the huge new American investments which had poured into these lands after World War II, guaranteed by the intimate alliance of investors and local power elite, would probably have been buried under the nationalist wave.

Awareness of the new people power thus created more confusion than clarity among American policymakers. On one hand, the Soviet Union was seen moving rapidly into the vast majority upheavals, turning the force of that swelling tide against the United States; on the other hand, American business and military bases abroad were built on the alliance with the minority-group rulers against whom the popular upheavals were directed. Pragmatic policy for the day, therefore, dictated actions in support of the alliances with minority groups and dictatorships, in the absence of any substitute policy which could protect immediate American overseas interests; at the same time, belated recognition of the overwhelming force of the "people movement" introduced a conflict in perception of reality, reflected in an over-all policy of confusion.

The new policy of confusion, however, was dumped into an attractive package. The new emphasis was to be on "democratization" of the minority power cliques, a vast project for turning hereditary wolves into bell-wethers to lead their flocks along the path of alliance with Uncle Sam and to protect them from the luring "baas" of Soviet Judas goats. Uncle Sam, as the shepherd, would pour sheep fodder into the feed lot to build up a contented flock, digging deep into his horn of plenty.

To "implement" the policy, the United States prepared to revise two traditional implements, its intelligence services and its propaganda agency, and to build a new "weapon" to take care of recalcitrant sheep which might not want to follow the new-model bellwethers and would insist on seeking greener pastures under their own leaders. The intelligence agency, it was presumed, would report the facts for each area on which specific policy could be based; the propaganda agency, in turn, would acquaint the local inhabitants with the essential goodness of their regime and its ally, the United States, while arousing natural antipathies to the Soviet Union and the Communist serpents loosed by it in the new Garden of Eden; and the new "weapon," baptized "The Little War," and equipped with a bag of tricks presumably gathered from the folk-war leaders and "improved on," would answer fire with fire whenever the alarm rang. We shall discuss these instruments in the next three chapters; they deserve attention.

The package was artfully streamlined. The content appeared logical and even pragmatic. However, in preparation of the answer, the problem had been forgotten; it had been, not how to shore up dictatorships, but how to go with, rather than against, the tides of majority upheaval and take the overbalancing people power out of Soviet hands. None of the three instruments was equipped for that basic task.

Nevertheless, the revised policy, despite intrinsic contradiction, could conceivably serve for a transition period—transition from all-out warfare against the tide of majority upheaval to gradual redeployment to the side of the people, via the palliative of "democratization from the top down." It is not wholly impossible that such a policy, if concretely put into practice through close control over minority power cliques in each area of upheaval, could stave off majority risings long enough for the switch in sides to be made. Democracy, of course, cannot be imposed from the top; as American school children used to learn, it has to come up from the people through the people's own representatives. However, close control over the dictator groups and our own investors (not impossible) might enable enough benefits to seep down to the people, even from existing regimes, to keep them quiet for a short while, perhaps long enough for a degree of transition to be made.

Unfortunately, as we shall see, none of the three policy instruments the United States hoped to use in the endeavor could serve to advance such a transition. In their existing forms, neither our intelligence service nor our propaganda agency was equipped to reach to the people of the upheaval lands, either to obtain facts on which to base policy, or to present facts as a means of carrying out policy. The tentative third instrument, the so-called "Little War," not only had limited practical value, but, in use, as the Cuban rehearsal showed, could cause far more loss of "people power" than it could gain in what might be called "geographic strategy."

More and more, it became clear to trained observers that if the United States hoped to move out of its policy blind alley—which seemed to be leading it consistently toward national decline and eventual defeat—it first of all had to revise its policy instruments and somehow make them effective within the new circumstances of stalemate, in which the balance could be maintained at all points except one, which had been left by default to Soviet manipulation. Obviously, in such circumstances, the stalemate was serving strictly

Soviet interests; yet there was no feasible way to break it.

The dilemma pointed up the fact that our intelligence service, as a policy instrument, had been extraordinarily ineffective, for reasons shown in Chapter 7. It was obvious that in the development of foreign policy, for any purpose except continual defeat, there could be no substitute for knowledge of the truth, including facts and meanings, as a policy guide; even actions aimed at countering the truth must take it into consideration. American foreign policy was confused, ineffective and at times counter-productive because policy-makers had no access to the truth, to facts and meanings, concerning the great underdeveloped areas of the world, the key regions of actual or potential folk war. Without such access, American policy was obliged to become a by-product of wishful thinking, assumptions and the geeing and hawing of private, rather than national, interest.

A second instrument, our information agency, as the propaganda arm of our foreign policy, suffered from two sides. Unable to obtain the facts about the underdeveloped areas because of biased reporting by our intelligence services, it was unable to place its propaganda within an acceptable framework, unable to put it into the terms of reference required for each area of penetration. Its task was made impossible, on the other side, by the nature of the American alliance with minority cliques; because it had to work through them, it was colored by them and its words became anathema among the majority out-groups. As will be shown in Chapter 8, this happened despite a remarkable technical efficiency.

The third proposed instrument of policy, the Little War, to be discussed in Chapter 9, was essentially a confession of failure in the use of the other two instruments. Military enforcement of policy always implies failure or incapacity in the use of nonmilitary means of enforcement; the Little War, however, as an instrument, assured failure through outright antagonism of people, the new strategic leverage. It could conceivably have some practical value under limited circumstances, as a means of answering unconventional military penetration by Russian, Chinese or other *foreign* forces into the upheaval areas. Such penetration, however, has not taken place thus far outside of American propaganda; and if it were undertaken, then genuine war, unlikely to stay "little," would in all likelihood ensue.

Because of the key importance of these three instruments of policy, a thorough look at each of them is advisable, without regard for sacrosanctity. There is not much time left for America to muddle along with instruments of policy which do not function and in their present form still would not function, even if our policy, through some miraculous insight unrelated to our defective instruments, were suddenly to become perfect.

> Fantasy and misconception obscure the truth and are certainly a disservice to scientific inquiry.
>
> — *Crawford H. Greenewalt*
>
> Speech at Princeton University, March, 1961.

7

Espionage, a Policy Key

When the Soviet Union made the balance of power wobble through its manipulation of selected majority movements in the upheaval areas, American policy-makers did not know how to respond. One reason was that they knew nothing about the upheaval areas except what the imperiled local minority cliques, with considerable self-censorship and self-interest, happened to tell them. The Soviet maneuver made intelligence-gathering in the upheaval lands extraordinarily urgent for the United States; without correct knowledge of developments there it would be impossible to form correct policies to offset the unbalancing Soviet thrusts.

When it became clear that something had to be

done, the policy-makers sent out a call for facts, even though they might be distasteful. They soon found that while we had innumerable intelligence agents, we had no reliable intelligence, as distinguished from opinion or one-sided data, about folk movements in areas of upheaval. There were three categories of sources of information, but all three suffered from grave defects. One, the economic or business reports filtered through the Department of Commerce, tended to be factual but by its nature limited and one-sided. Another, the written accounts of American and foreign newsmen, culled from publications, was superficial. The third source, espionage, on which governments from time immemorial have relied, suffered from a basic flaw that merits thorough analysis.

American intelligence mechanisms have been extraordinarily complicated in comparison with their British or Soviet counterparts. At the time of their "agonizing reappraisal," in May and June of 1961, there were the Central Intelligence Agency (CIA), set up under Federal statute in 1947 as "an instrument of presidential policy," under Allen W. Dulles since 1953; the Office of Naval Intelligence; an Army G-2; an Airforce A-2; the Joint Intelligence Group of the Joint Staff of the Joint Chiefs of Staff, affectionately called "the Joint"; the National Security Agency, with compartments for communications, codes, ciphers and a sort of one-man bureau with committees, Major General Graves B. Erskine, linking it with Secretary of Defense and branching out, on the way, into security, unconventional warfare and psychological warfare; also, the Federal Bureau of Investigation to help out with counterespionage; the State Department's special intelligence group; still another operating under the Atomic Energy Committee; then, not quite finally, the Intelligence Advisory Committee headed by Allen W. Dulles, possibly in an effort to close the circle. The last-named group theoretically included heads or representatives of all other agencies, except two or three utterly hush-hush set-ups, and met weekly whenever a big enough hall was available. The interminable but still incomplete list of agencies and subagencies (a special eight-man Presidential Board was also set up in 1956) was complicated enough in itself; however, a main problem, apart from coordination, was that each grouplet tended to emphasize its own activity keeping one eye on the budget. An evaluation without this special angle was rare.

Largely because of Dulles' position as head of the CIA and the Advisory Committee, much of the burden and the blame for the entire intelligence operation fell on his shoulders. As a technician, however, friend and foe recognized that he did yeoman work, although by no means herculean. It was a little known fact that Dulles was at all times under political control; mistakes "made by the CIA" in such matters as the U-2 incident or the Cuban or Laotian fiascos first had to be approved, under the enabling statute of 1947, by the President himself. Dulles' main difficulty was inherent in the basic flaw in American foreign policy, its essential determination by overseas business interests; as a man with, at one time, wide investor interests himself, particularly in Germany, he naturally sympathized with investors' problems. The close link between CIA actions in Iran, Guatemala and Cuba and the parallel actions of American investors there, was by no means coincidental; however, Dulles erred no more in this respect than the entire body of American policy-makers, subject as they were to but one major pressure group. Dulles, according to fairly reliable reports, flirted with the idea of finding "people bases" as substitutes for the weakening dictatorships among our allies. An example cited has been the tentative flirtation that took place between the CIA and men close to Fidel Castro prior to the collapse of the Batista dictatorship. The absence of firm policy on top, in the Executive, may have been one explanation for irresolute CIA actions along this line.

With the binding limitations of poorly based and poorly defined policy, and the one-sidedness inherent in major control by a single pressure group, American intelligence activities were necessarily of poor quality. Data obtained were not only frequently inaccurate, as in the cases of the Russian hydrogen bomb, the Red Chinese entry into Korea, the Hungarian debacle, Russian rocketry advances, and so on, some of them involving grave danger to the nation; for reasons to be explained these data were at times exactly the opposite of the truth and were a serious factor in causing American policy at times to be diametrically wrong. The failure was evident whenever American foreign policy attempted to counteract the Soviet tactics of using people as a power-base in the upheaval areas.

An intelligence agency worth its salt does one main job: It finds the facts and the primary meanings of any development, large or small, which might in any way affect the national interests of its home country. Its agents should have no opinions at all, preferably, except for such interpretative addenda as might be necessary to attach, separately, to the facts as learned. Evaluation of facts should take place at headquarters, after all pertinent data have been gathered, by experts so skilled in their area of specialization that they have almost an intuition of the pattern the facts take as they shape together. These experts must be dual-minded; they must think at the same time in American terms and in the subtly different terms of psychological reference that make sense in the area from which the data come. They must know, for example, that if a popular leader in an underdeveloped area attacks "imperialists" he is not necessarily a Communist or even anti-American. "Imperialists," to the popular leader, might mean any foreign investors allied to the minority power elite in his country.

Intelligence thus consists of two basic operations: Accurate fact-gathering; accurate evaluation. Neither can serve without the other. Accurate intelligence gives a country a firm basis on which to build foreign policy—conditioned, of course, by its capability to carry it out. Inaccurate intelligence will almost always lead to a foreign policy that will not advance national interests.

Because of American failures in the effort to counterbalance the Soviet "people base" of power, the Central Intelligence Agency was a frequent target of attack. The attacks, however, were not aimed at its essential flaw; they dodged all around it. There was very little wrong with the information-gathering *structure* of the CIA; even its much criticized but overstated secrecy was a necessary condition of efficiency and accuracy in espionage which needed to be made more effective, not less. The flaw that counted was of a different kind. It lay with its personnel.

It will be recalled that in the early 1950's, not too

74

long after the CIA began to function, the United States entered an era of ideological panic, a fear-and-confusion reaction engendered domestically by attempts to lift the nuclear Fantasy Curtain and on a world level by the visible expansion of Communist influence into areas left open by the retreat into nuclear unreality. During the panic, government agencies were indiscriminately purged of non-rightists, particularly nonconforming "leftists" of the Roosevelt tradition. Although only a few hundred, usually charged with being Communists, were dismissed outright, many thousands quietly resigned from government service, disgusted by harassment or by the growing domination of extreme right-wingers. Agency heads, many of them aware that fantasy was involved, bent over backward to keep "clean," fearing their own political futures.

In the panic period and thereafter, the prerequisite for employment in the Central Intelligence Agency came to be either a spotless record of conformism or a baptismal certificate in the Roman Catholic Church, which was presumed to be a guarantee against "leftism." Overseas, almost all CIA agents who had been associated with the O.S.S. or other wartime agencies were dropped. In their stead were hired individuals of "known anti-Communist" background. Unfortunately, in practice, these persons tended to be either former Axis collaborators or members of extreme right-wing clerical movements.

With its new personnel, the CIA administrators felt safe against the onslaughts of American politicians; but they no longer had an intelligence agency to administer. The new employees emotionally divided the world into "Red" and "White." They saw Communists behind every movement of the common people. They tended to form opinions, then look exclusively for data to back them up. Irrational data were forwarded at times, particularly material obtained from casualties of ideological conflict in Central Europe, many of whom were employed as informants, or even placed in policy positions; the "brains" of the American fiasco in Cuba in 1961, for example, was a German. Native American field employees of the CIA, products of a selection system which put a premium on callowness, were easily maneuvered by the extremists.

Many of the reports that began to flow to CIA were merely leftover materials from Axis wartime surplus. In many cases, the original sources were the same persons who had been informants of the Axis espionage network, particularly, in Latin America, of the Falange operation which had been paid for via the Nazi *Fichtebund*, and, in Asia, of the "Saibatsu" business group of Imperial Japan. New information, in the underdeveloped areas, was obtained exclusively from the local power elite, eager to provoke direct or indirect American intervention against the rising majorities. The bias was built in.

The effect was not only on the accuracy of data. The known right-wing fanaticism of many CIA agents and informants prevented them from necessary assumption of protective coloration; but Soviet agents moved easily into the CIA network, putting on facile veneers of quasi-fascism or passing themselves off as "refugees." The only password they needed was a "known anti-Communist" background, which any skilled agent could fabricate on his day off. The few unbiased employees left in the CIA for accurate checks on data or personnel were smothered into conformism and acceptance or hamstrung into inefficiency.

The swing toward what is called conservatism in the United States has made correction of the essential "personnel" flaw of the CIA even more difficult; but there is no doubt that unless it is corrected the United States cannot properly formulate a policy to offset Soviet moves from its base of "people power." Probably the only way corrective steps could be taken, under continuing circumstances of fantasy and fear, would be for American conservatives themselves, placing national safety above their presumed ideology, to do the job. Otherwise, they would feel obliged to raise a hue and cry which would once again frighten agency heads.

An intelligence agency has to deal with conditions as they exist, particularly in times of rapid movement and wide upheaval, when significant change constantly occurs. It should be realized that although the United States, in its fear of Russia, has moved to the "right," the rest of the world, except for a few dependent dictatorships, has swung to the "left." In underdeveloped areas leaders of popular movements are often much farther left than local Communists, who may attack them as "infantile romantics." Many such leaders are almost as far left as Thomas Jefferson. Plainly, quasi-fascists and former Axis collaborators or hangers-on of minority-power cliques cannot provide really pertinent data concerning today's upheaval areas and their tidal wave of people. They are not in touch; and most data they might supply would merely add to an existing curtain of fantasy.

The peculiar quality of agents used by Central Intelligence even barred the United States from effective use of double agents, the operatives who work for both sides but on behalf of one, an area in which Allen W. Dulles was able to specialize, through select personnel, during his wartime operations in Switzerland. This device has now had to be left substantially to our British allies, who have their own national interests to serve. It is possible that a brief look at how this aspect of British intelligence might have functioned in one recent case, if coupled with high-level consultations between American intelligence chiefs and their British counterparts, could lead to improvement in the American system.

Because British professionals discovered a long time ago that mental conformists and cog-thinkers made poor operatives in the field, they have been able to make special and effective use of the double-agent device. To illustrate a possibility—strictly a possibility—of how skilled professionals operate in this area let us take the case of George Blake, an operative sentenced to forty-two years in prison by the British in early 1961 for passing secrets to the Russians. Blake, a fortyish, retiring sort, confessed in Old Bailey that he had been a Red sympathizer since 1951, after being "brainwashed" in a Korean prison camp, where he had been interned as British vice-counsel in Seoul. After release, from 1953 to 1960, Blake had worked directly with MI-6, Britain's crack international spy brigade.

Why did the Lord Chief Justice, passing sentence on Blake, tell him, "I fully recognize that it is unfortunate for you that many matters which may have urged mitigation were not divulgeable"? Why did Macmillan tell the House of Commons that Blake's action was "not the result of brainwashing," or that, if required, he would discuss the affair with the leader of the Opposition but only in the most complete confidence?

The Blake case indicated an interesting possibility for a professional intelligence service with personnel capable of functioning as double agents. A double agent, of all field operatives, is the most strategically valuable in that he can, after obtaining the enemy's trust by passing on to them a few well-chosen secrets, be used to plant material that will lead the enemy to make wrong decisions at crucial times. After a few such actions, however, the coincidence will be observed and the double agent will become suspect. At that point, since no chances can be taken, the enemy "sacrifices" him by arranging for his exposure as their agent. The reaction will give them the clue to the validity of the material; if the double agent is arrested as a spy and dealt with harshly, the material is valid; he really was with them. The next step, of course, is for the country planting the information to be sure to arrest and deal harshly with its own faithful agent; in that way the validity of the material, vital to the success of over-all strategy, appears guaranteed. A sentence three times that given to Klaus Fuchs, for example, would seem sufficiently harsh for the purpose.

Of course, if a double agent really defected, as Blake is said to have done, then grave problems would be created for the intelligence service. For example, in Blake's case, Britain's entire MI-6 operation, almost around the world, would have been reshuffled, agents changed, and new covers built. Hundreds of British informants in areas controlled by the Communist bloc would have been thrown in jail or choked with shadows. Fortunately, a collapse of this nature of MI-6 functions has never, so far, been a problem for British intelligence.

The foregoing, of course, should be considered pure speculation, as a means of exploring possibilities available to British intelligence, because of the make-up of their personnel, but not available on a similar level for the United States.

British intelligence, to be sure, starts off with an advantage because of the traditional unity of executive and legislative functions; there is little cross-purpose. Also, the heads are all "members," in the British way, of the same "old school-tie set," unobliged to be conformists, without political rivalry, trustful of each other, able to synchronize at a second's notice. Their work is shielded behind the Official Secrets Act, extraordinarily effective as a barrier, and all the more so because, for the press, it is essentially voluntary.

Secret "political" work is sharply separated from military acts, with top secret undertakings under the direct control of a special Cabinet subcommittee. The heart is MI-5 and MI-6, controlled by civilians directly under the Prime Minister. MI-5 is mainly a counter-intelligence and screening agency. The most important work of MI-6, at present, is the direction of intelligence activities overseas, under conditions of inviolable secrecy. The British also have Navy, Army and Airforce intelligence units, more or less parallel to those of the United States; a special branch of Scotland Yard which investigates or picks up enemy agents, defectors and the like under tight control by MI-5; and an over-all collating agency, the Joint Intelligence Bureau with a committee of fifty. In 1961 this committee was under Sir Kenneth Strong, who reported to the Minister of Defense or, in ultrasecret circumstances, to Prime Minister Macmillan.

A distinguishing characteristic of British intelligence, compared with American, is the freedom of movement inside it, and the absolute tightness of secrecy around it; perhaps no more than five hundred Britons, for example, know details of the guarded liaison between MI-6 and the Foreign Office, where the factual elements of Britain's foreign policy are put together. The most distinguishing characteristic of all is the cultivated and disciplined avoidance of preconceptions or bias which mark both field agents and evaluation experts.

This has been a key difference between the British and American operations. To a degree, the biases of CIA agents and their tendency to submit highly colored or even false data, had an effect on American intelligence operations like that of a network of efficient Russian double agents. If the Executive, instead of relying on CIA information, had taken the opposite direction each time, then on the basis of past performance, American foreign policy would have been more often right than wrong. Meanwhile, access to facts and meanings concerning the upheaval areas was effectively barred; and the United States had no basis on which to form a policy of "people" to offset that of the Soviet Union.

Gathering facts for policy formation is far more important at the moment for the United States than "fancy" espionage. Our primary problems come from lack of knowledge, as shown by the Cuban fiasco, among many others. Access to truth must be the first objective in seeking solutions. For access to the truth, the United

States must have accurate sources of information. If its present sources are inaccurate, it requires new ones.

In the complicated and changing world of folk war and unrest, an intelligence agency must be much more than the old-fashioned spy ring described in Sunday supplements. To military and economic data must be added "people" data on a scale never dreamed of by "propaganda warfare" experts. Intelligence gathering has become, essentially, scientific research work, along the lines being tried on a small scale by Britain's MI-6. Intelligence does not consist of repeating fairy stories such as the reports, duly filed by CIA, of "Russian rocket bases" in Cuba. A functioning intelligence agency, receiving such reports, would have checked them out. The duty of a spy is in no way related to making propaganda, except to the degree that professional propagandists may be able to calculate their work on the basis of his truthful reports. False information has no place in espionage; it will tend to be the result of either inexcusable ineptness or evidence of counteragent activity.

The great U-2 blooper, which helped precipitate the downhill slide of American prestige so far as our reputation for veracity was concerned, had far more significance as a revelation of inefficiency in espionage than as an example of "brinkmanship." The fact that such a grave risk would be taken merely to obtain intelligence data showed the world that we had no intelligence mechanism functioning reliably inside the Soviet Union to do the job as it should be done.

The cause of American ineptness was sometimes ascribed to the "secrecy" of the Soviet Union, China, the majority movements of Southeast Asia or Africa, or even Cuba, in fact, of any world area where our agents are not welcomed with open arms. Secrecy, however, far from being an excuse for poor espionage, provides an ideal climate for gathering intelligence data. It means that all key information has already been put together and labeled for the agent. All he has to do is to be cleared for access to it—something far easier for a skilled operative, with his carefully built-up cover, than for any one else. So-called "iron-clad" secrecy is almost made to order for espionage penetration. The protective routines, the identification red tape, and all the rest of it provide an easy pattern for the spy to adapt himself to without suspicion.

The poor functioning of CIA agents in such ideal conditions came from their characteristics as noted. Ultra-rightist fanatics almost to a man, they had already exposed themselves as eccentric characters and suspicious persons in every country except possibly Spain, Portugal and a few Asian or Latin American dictatorships, where they had easy access to government data— but no access to the potential rulers in the majority popular movements. CIA personnel were not even as effective as routine newspaper correspondents. Three weeks before the Chinese moved across the Yalu River in response to MacArthur's drive against their frontier, the Chinese decision to do so was widely reported in the British press. While American agents in Laos were reporting vast incursions of foreign Communists into that "bastion of freedom" and the Pentagon was mobilizing for counterattack, a routine correspondent for the *Wall Street Journal* casually reported that no foreigners were among the Pathet Lao forces—in fact, few Communists of any kind. Some days later, the United States backtracked once again. The examples ran into hundreds; and it seemed that if common ordinary newspapermen could casually obtain facts beyond the reach of the CIA, something had to be wrong with CIA factfinders.

A growing American preoccupation with form rather than substance—as illustrated by professionally designed but unopenable packages or "streamlined" toasters—also had its effect on intelligence gathering. The dictatorships in Spain or Portugal or Southeast Asia or Latin America were, in form, on "our side"; therefore the popular opposition to them, even though it, in fact, might be the substance of the country, was against us; therefore it was "Communist" or "Red-led." The agrarian leader who decried, say, church ownership of most of his country's farmland, became "an atheistic Communist"; the anti-imperialist or nationalist or neutralist was "anti-American." Once these assumptions were made, even a nonbiased CIA operative, knowing the conditions of his job, would be foolhardy to send in data to the contrary, or even look for it. We let the popular movements go by default first, then attacked them. The Russians merely picked up the marbles at their leisure.

An intelligence agent must feel free to send in any data verified by him to the best of his ability. Let us oversimplify to make the point:

If an operative discovers that the elderly mother of a top Communist in lower Afrasia receives roses from her son every Monday night, he might report it as a matter of background; but he should not be required to transmute the roses, in his report, into vials of poison. If he learns that 5,000 peasants have taken the field against a local dictatorship, he should not feel obliged to describe them as invading Communists merely because the dictator says they are. These examples are not exaggerations. Similar reports were channeled to American intelligence every day, only some of them as plants by counteragents. Most reports of this type were seriously made by operatives who might even have believed them to be true.

For extreme problems, solutions may have to be extreme: To enable the United States to regain its balance in its policy tug-of-war with the Soviet Union, one step, an important one, in the right direction would be to replace such CIA personnel, from top to bottom. Instead of present fanatics and naïve incompetents, skilled professionals should be recruited, without bias or preconception so far as humanly possible. Emphasis should be placed on selection of men and women schooled in the pertinent sciences, and also in language, psychology and human relations. Espionage itself is becoming a science in which quacks, crackpots or fanatics have no direct value.

So that desperately needed facts about the world of upheaval could be obtained swiftly, it became obvious that another step would be to take responsibility for "paramilitary" operations out of CIA hands; and a constructive decision to this effect was made in 1961 by U. S. authorities. An espionage agency, if it is to gather facts from sources that may not want to tell everybody or may not want their informant role known, has to be secret, not merely by definition in regulations, but in fact; its agents must have "cover." An intelligence operative should be a research scientist with special qualifications not too frequently encountered; he should not be an adolescent waving a bomb.

Experience during the past decade also seems to indicate that during the period of re-formation, until efficiency in evaluation is also restored, the functions of the CIA should be largely limited to fact-gathering. Evaluation, even primary evaluation, might best be made the concern, for the time being, of a separate board of specialists in world areas of American concern, men and women directly under the President, who would know intimately their special world areas and, above all, the majorities in them. Such a board could evaluate data as gathered, passing back to intelligence for immediate re-check those items which might require it.

Fortunately the corrective measures needed by the CIA, though perhaps embarrassing to contemplate, are not too difficult to apply. The personnel change would have to take place before any significant success could be attained by the United States in the new areas of foreign policy, the areas of people. Until that is done, the United States will tend to be a nation of the blind attempting to lead a relatively sighted world, a world moving in a direction opposite to the one our "intelligence experts" too often have indicated.

We've got to face the truth without any compromises, regardless of how unpleasant some may find it.

— *A. Whitney Griswold*

Talk at Yale Alumni
luncheon, June 18, 1961.

8

For Righteous or Sinners

In considering the effectiveness of the American propaganda instrument as a means of carrying out a phase of foreign policy in the areas of upheaval, it might not be amiss to recall a favorite quotation of Jeffersonian Americans, whose early upheaval turned out quite well despite the existence of a foreign-linked power elite. Although only one in seventeen of those earlier Americans was a church member, many were assiduous Bible readers. In that Book they found what today would be called "a statement of policy" which American propagandists might consider:

"I came not to call the righteous but the sinners to repentance."

Along with the rush toward church membership has come a parallel modern decline in Bible reading, which may help explain modern aversion to many early American precepts. Our propaganda, to the extent it has taken people into consideration at all, has been aimed strictly at leading the "righteous," that is, the ones already on "our side," for economic reasons, to a presumed salvation; the 90 per cent, the huge out-group majorities in the underdeveloped lands, who are "sinners" in our eyes, have been left for the Soviet Union to manipulate or, at least, to infiltrate.

This is particularly so in the critical areas of upheaval, where the existing power cliques are strongly supported by us and laved by high-powered propaganda, while the huge popular movements, although really brought into being by Western economic organization, are forcibly opposed, even by armed intervention, and left unilluminated by our message. This apparently enigmatic propaganda policy, which would seem to be directed at building another barrier against the earth turning, is in fact logical and even inevitable, given the limited premise on which it is built.

As has been noted, and as we shall see more fully in Chapter 10, American foreign policy and therefore its propaganda arm is determined by the Executive branch of the government, subject to important influence by only one major pressure group, our overseas investors. American propaganda thus tends automatically to serve primarily the interests of the dominant group concerned; and the interest of this group, quite logically and praiseworthily, is to sell goods and services and make profits abroad.

What could be less enigmatic, therefore, than a propaganda policy aimed at the "righteous," at the 10 per cent in the underdeveloped areas who have wealth and purchasing power? Could one expect it to be aimed at the 90 per cent who cannot buy? Advertising men, who are commercial propagandists, discovered long ago that if you want to sell something, you make your pitch to the customer with purchasing power, not to someone who is dead broke. The motivation in American propaganda, and much of its content, is thus commercial—and effective within those limits.

Unfortunately, in the confusion between long-range national interests and short-range business interests, our propagandists were unable to recognize that the two do not always coincide. What is good for General Motors in the short run may not be good for the country in the long run. The balance of power in the whole of the underdeveloped world is swinging over rapidly from the 10 per cent to the 90 per cent; and as power goes, so goes the wealth of the nation, including whatever share in it American overseas investors might have.

American propaganda, along with the military and economic instruments of our foreign policy, suffers from the lack of "people power" and "people objective." It is essentially class propaganda; we save the saved and convert the converted. Long before we became so powerful, we did a better job in reaching the people. Our own revolution was the mother of the first great wave of upheaval; all through the late eighteenth and the entire nineteenth centuries documents such as our Dec-

89

laration of Independence and the Bill of Rights were smuggled from popular leader to popular leader; the great Brazilian patriot Tiradentes was reputedly hanged because a copy of the Declaration of Independence was found in his pocket. Even today the words of Thomas Jefferson, forgotten (and some of them considered subversive) in his homeland, come easily to the tongues of the leaders of the submerged peoples in many lands, quoted often to refute our present-day propaganda.

The advanced, streamlined, efficient and modern techniques used by our principal propaganda agency, the United States Information Service (an agency at home, USIA; a service overseas, USIS) must be applied, unfortunately, in areas of upheaval where the local population has not been conditioned to them by Madison Avenue commercials. Laos was a case in point. It was a critical area; hundreds of millions of American dollars had poured into the tiny Buddhist country until the officials of the United States-sponsored regime had accumulated so many luxury cars that more millions had to be sent to build roads for them. The USIS also had available in Laos, because of the emergency circumstances, a much larger allocation than usual; it had enough funds to do whatever the job might require over a critical period.

The first problem faced by USIS was a common one in the upheaval areas: Not more than one out of six Laotians could read; few had radios; none had television. As a noble gesture, however, the USIS turned out something like one million leaflets and pamphlets, forty-eight different varieties, on a specially imported, late-model printing plant. American planes dropped them over the countryside among the peasants, warning them against the Pathet Lao, the folk-war movement, and lauding the U.S.-sponsored regime in Vientiane, whose representatives 90 per cent of the local peasantry had never seen. The leaflets were turned out by a staff of seventeen Americans and seventy-two Filipinos, Thais and Vietnamese—no Laotians. Laotians were used by USIS for menial jobs only; skilled Laotians were either unavailable or preferred not to get mixed up with the American effort.

It did not take long, however, for USIS, using approved market-survey techniques similar to those employed by McCann-Erickson for its overseas business clients, to discover a degree of difficulty in reaching an illiterate population with its kind of literature. It soon decided to concentrate on movie shorts and features. A total of eighty-three films were prepared for Laotian audiences. Worked in with the subject matter were carefully prepared eulogies of the U.S.-sponsored regime of Prince Boun Oum and devastating attacks on the Pathet Lao movement as Communist.

In at least one of these commentaries the Pathet Lao were presented as possessed of "evil spirits." They were Laotian outside, the film admitted, but inside they were evil spirits who, in accordance with the injunction against allowing witches to live, should be done away with forthwith. This was received with some doubt by the audiences, most of whom were themselves Pathet Lao sympathizers, as evidence of American superstitions foreign to Buddhism. One film, which showed up-to-date American methods of chicken farming, achieved success in the village of Na Nong Buk, near Vientiane. The peasantry was much impressed with the chicken-housing, considerably better than their own; but the commentary to the effect that the Pathet Lao, if they took over, would ban private chicken raising, was received with some wonder. The Pathet Lao had already taken over; every male in the village, most of them chicken owners, was already in the movement except for three new officials sent from Vientiane who had no chickens.

An especially prized film defined communism which the Laotians had not heard of. "What is it?" the girl heroine asked her boy friend, a stalwart friend of the United States. "Well," the young hero replied, "if I cut my hand off and then make everybody else do the same thing, that's communism." "Oh," commented the heroine, "how frightful is communism." Silly as this sounds, it was an attempt to put across a common *American* idea of communism, that is, a conspiracy by people who have nothing, to take away the possessions of those who have something. In the United States or among Laotian wealthy, this might have been an acceptable, although infantile, definition; among Laotian villagers, even if they understood the implication it would have meant little. They had nothing to lose under any "ism."

The key reason for failure of the "all-out" USIS effort in Laos, however, lay in its basic orientation. This was defined by a top American official on the scene. "Our main effort in Laos," he said, "is to tell the people about their own good government (our Prince Boun Oum regime) and about the dangers of communism."

Even if the United States at one time had a chance in Laos—doubtful at best in view of the side we were on—this orientation would have killed the chance. The first rule in propaganda, when an unpopular government must be praised to its own antagonistic people, is to try to get a popular local figurehead to do the praising; for a foreign agency to do so automatically heightens the antagonism. Just why a group of foreigners should tell a doubtful people how wonderful their own government is, or how bad their fellow citizens are, is a question which has only one answer: The doubtful government is linked with the foreigners. This, of course, was the propaganda objective in Laos, not of USIS, but of the anti-American Pathet Lao. The aim of the Pathet Lao was to paint Prince Boun Oum as a puppet of American imperialists; the USIS achieved the Pathet Lao objective.

Endless poring over of Madison Avenue propaganda techniques by Communist agents could not have produced a better method for the Pathet Lao than the one devised by the USIS in all its innocence. It may be a good thing that most of the upheaval areas have still not been subjected to a "crash program" of American propaganda; the Pathet Lao might now be worldwide.

Apart from propaganda objectives, however, the Laotian fiasco pointed up an aspect of propaganda content. The plain fact was that Prince Boun Oum, however honest, capable or patriotic, was indeed at the time an American puppet, installed by the United States after deposition of a legitimate government—legitimate, that is, in Laotian terms. To presume that any people, even the most illiterate and naïve, would not recognize that fact, indicates a contempt for people by American officialdom, an assumption that American powers of enforcement of policy are so great that people need not

93

be considered. Once again, the basic flaw was demonstrated.

Propaganda, like war, is merely one means of carrying out foreign policy, of trying to impose that policy on others. Success in propaganda, as in war, depends on the use of power (words) at the right time, in the right place, in the right amount and in the right way. In propaganda, as in war, a key element in success is to know the enemy as well as yourself—by no means an easy knowledge to attain—and to know your allies. Words are the weapons in propaganda; but words, unlike bombs, are not necessarily the same for all men.

Propaganda, no matter how true or false, passes through the filter of man's mind; and in the passage it may come to have a wholly different meaning. American lack of knowledge of how and what the great majorities feel and think in the areas of upheaval—a lack directly traceable to the make-up of our intelligence organization—has rendered our propaganda peculiarly ineffective and even counterproductive among these masses of people, quite apart from its basic flaw, derived from its orientation and content.

An expert propagandist, given a free hand, can convince most people that any object not in their visual range is white instead of dark gray and still adhere strictly to the "truth." He does this by first building in his audience a desire to learn that the object is white, and second, by abstracting from the dark gray its white content and presenting it as white. The technique is easily understood in terms of people: An individual will have, say, four good points, ten bad points and six neutral points; but an expert propagandist can make this mostly bad person seem extraordinarily and humanly good by stressing his four good points and lightly mentioning one or two neutral points for apparent balance. But the technique will work only if this good-bad person is beyond the checking range of the audience. If they see him and know him, the propaganda will immediately be called fake and will backfire. Even if the audience only believes it sees him and knows him as bad, the propaganda will fail.

Propaganda, in other words, must take into account the existing image in a man's mind; it cannot brainwash—this is an individual, not a mass approach. The existing image can be changed somewhat; in some cases a similar but intrinsically different image can be superimposed; but the image cannot be wholly extirpated within the limits of one generation.

This is why American propagandists, no matter how efficiently they try, cannot convince the submerged majorities in the areas of upheaval that the ruling group in their land is good. The existing image is one of a group of corrupt oppressors and overlords; shifts of power within the ruling group, by *coups d'etat* or otherwise, may change the image somewhat; in a few cases another image has been superimposed; but the memory remains and the facts of poverty, disease and exploitation remain. No propaganda can effectively counteract an existing and obvious fact.

To the degree that American businessmen and, through them, America, are associated with the existing image of an exploiting power group, the majorities in the underdeveloped lands will associate America with that group, regardless of propaganda. Before their eyes the people see the American standing at the side of their corrupt rulers; they may even see him calling on his government to bring in planes and guns to save the minority clique from the majority rising. The image and the fact render worthless any contrary propaganda, however suave.

The importance of the existing image is illustrated also by the strictly relative success of American propaganda in the more developed countries, particularly those peopled or culturally dominated by Western Europeans or their descendants. American withdrawal into nuclear fantasy, the failure to obtain facts and meanings as a basis for policy and its propaganda arm, even mistakes such as the Cuban fiasco, could not wholly erase the image of America that had been built up among these people. In those areas, American propaganda, no matter how poor in content, was filtered through minds which saw America as a land of promise, where kinfolk lived or had gone long before. We were scoffed at by Western Europeans, called childish, or, more pointedly, dreamers, materialists, even warmongers, but the old image of America was still there to transmute the new impressions.

Even in the developed countries of Western European culture, however, American propaganda tends to succeed or fail along class lines; conservative businessmen and most of the middle class are with us; most of the lower-middle class and the urban or rural working people are against us, although hesitantly. The split is sharply illustrated in Brazil, a country which contains one of the world's most highly developed areas, centering around São Paulo, and one of the world's most backward areas in the Northeast. The people of São Paulo, for the most part, think of Americans almost exactly in

Western European terms; the people of the Northeast, except for the tiny, exploiting power clique, typical of areas of upheaval, have an attitude almost like that of pro-Castro Cubans.

For the "sinners," for the roughly two-thirds of the earth's population who live in the underdeveloped lands of Asia, Africa and Latin America, the out-groups, our road to salvation seems both hypothetical and hypocritical. Our propaganda has not diminished the interfering image; on the contrary, by the reactive process which obvious falsehood generates, we have magnified it. By our deeds they know us. We can, if we want to, change the deeds; that, after all, is the first step in good "public relations." The second step is to explain our deeds in their terms, not ours, which means that we must first learn how they think and feel.

Soviet propaganda, technically, is far inferior to American. In the underdeveloped areas not yet overrun by folk war, the United States makes use of newspaper, radio and television outlets for its propaganda at a ratio of approximately 500 for any one available to the Soviet Union. Many of the smaller newspapers in Latin America, Asia and even Africa are so swamped with news and feature releases distributed by the United States Information Agency that the local news staff uses the backs for copy paper, a sizable saving in areas where paper is expensive. Few of these outlets have even been offered official Soviet propaganda; and practically none of them would use it if it were offered. Moreover, USIA propaganda is widely printed and broadcast, although not because of intrinsic interest. It is used for the same reason that a newspaper in the United States, angling for or receiving a big advertisement from a major company, will tend to run news stories about that company. This tendency does not imply direct pressure by the advertiser; it is a more or less "unconscious recognition" of which side of the bread is buttered. American foreign investors and their local representatives, with commendable patriotism, tend to place their advertising with those news outlets which use American propaganda and tend to throw political and economic favors to their owners.

In every technical way, America's official propaganda machinery works far more smoothly than any other. The United States Information Agency, although it may appear amateurish to professional newspapermen or in comparison with major news agencies, is the most efficient propaganda service ever developed, so far as operational procedures go. Propaganda flows smoothly from New York and Washington and local centers overseas to publications around the world. *Official* Soviet propaganda, distributed mostly through the Tass agency, uses techniques which seem almost juvenile in comparison.

Why, then, at every point of critical competition, has Soviet propaganda outpulled the American variety?

There have, of course, been "bad breaks" for American propaganda, such as the U-2 incident, the Cuban fiasco, and the Russian Sputnik or man-in-orbit beats. Of these, however, only the Cuban fiasco was deeply damaging to American interests in the underdeveloped lands; the others did not really have everyday meaning for the masses of people. Bad breaks can come in any propaganda war; they can be overcome. It is not on this level, despite isolated, flashy victories, that Soviet propaganda is winning.

Consistently, American propaganda has met defeat on the "people" level; it cannot penetrate the majorities in the underdeveloped areas and has been especially ineffective among those in or near upheaval. In those areas where the people see Americans aligned with their enemy, the people themselves carry on propaganda which contains much that is anti-American and much that is pro-Soviet or pro-Chinese. Their propaganda is principally word-of-mouth, the age-old method native to the area; but the general illiteracy has not prevented an extraordinarily wide distribution of tiny, four-page pamphlets, handbills and one-sheet newspapers, written simply and plainly in the terms of the average peasant or workman. Where illiteracy is almost total, someone will volunteer to read the contents to small or large groups. Included in this "literature" are millions of copies of tiny pamphlets smuggled in from the Soviet Union and China and distributed and read, not by Russians or Chinese in air-conditioned information offices, but by unpaid native men and women.

In thousands of rural villages throughout the upheaval areas of the world, half-literate peasants are even poring over the complicated writings of Mao, idiomatically translated. In Latin America, groups have actually gathered to study a rather simple description of a phase of guerrilla warfare written by Ernesto Guevara—indications are that some 100,000 copies have been distributed there, although hardly a bookstore displays them. Why American propaganda fails lies basically in its support of the minority groups, but it fails also because it ignores the problems of change and offers no

99

solutions except a glorified status quo. Even without the interfering image of American business linked with the local power clique, American propaganda could not compete.

Technical facility cannot make up for content; access to the press, radio and television of the ruling clique in the underdeveloped areas does not equal access to the hearts and minds of the people; and, if an old saying may be misquoted, propaganda without works is dead. If we want the people of the underdeveloped world to go with us, we have to go with them, both in words and deeds.

Once again, American technique has produced a pretty package; but it doesn't open for the consumer to get at the contents. Those who accept American propaganda do so because they are already on our side for economic reasons. Those who do not accept it are already against us or at best doubtful of us, for reasons which are also economic in essence.

Our propaganda—like our "little war" ideas, our foreign investors, our intelligence agency, and our entire inchoate foreign policy—goes against the tide. As a "thing-in-itself," our propaganda machinery may be the most streamlined ever developed by artful man; but it is beyond the power of any propaganda to overcome the overwhelming weight of events that are overturning the age-old balances in the upheaval areas.

The effect of American propaganda has been almost as serious at home as overseas, possibly more so in some ways. In this respect American propaganda has, on the whole, had results "superior" to the Russian variety; it is at least believed domestically. No

100

press in the world, except perhaps in China, is as full of propaganda as the American—although the American lead over the Soviet Union in this respect is due to a technical fact: The American press is deluged not only with government propaganda and the angling of the wire services and local editors, but with handouts from private propagandists, flacks and public-relations firms and departments, all promoting some private interest. On a typical day, 75 to 85 per cent of all "news" in two New York afternoon papers was found to be either outright propaganda from one source or another or demonstrably angled—not counting advertisements, which of course are also propaganda of a sort.

It has been the American press, as a vehicle for propaganda—and with a tremendous assist from television—which has pounded home to a credulous public such Orwellian ideas as peace through war with Russia and China; freeing Cuba by conquest; increased defense expeditures through lower taxes; extending American influence by cutting foreign aid; expulsion from the United Nations of all nations not pro-American; Formosa is China; aid the needy by cutting relief; invade Laos to repel the Laotians; or even Civil Defense against Russian H-Bombs. A complete negation of reality was at times apparent in this propaganda—for example, a general refusal to believe that the Russians had sent a rocket around the moon or a spaceman into orbit. A surprising percentage of these strange unrealisms would seem to be accepted, as a result of the propaganda effort, by a majority of Americans in the metropolitan East and a sizable minority elsewhere.

These American fantasies, among others, have led many foreigners to wonder if Americans are either incredibly naïve or verging on a national nervous breakdown. In talking with American "believers," informed Englishmen have reported a sensation similar to that received in an attempt at logical conversation with a member of the world-is-flat sect. An American may test this peculiarity on himself by reading a European or even a Canadian newspaper after a steady diet of, say, the New York *Daily News*.

An indication that this danger of immersion of Americans in fantasy has caused some preoccupation among our policy-makers was contained in a talk in 1961 by President John F. Kennedy before the Society of Newspaper Editors. "The President of a great democracy such as ours," he said, "and the editors of great newspapers such as yours owe a common obligation to present the facts, and to present them with candor and to present them in perspective."

There are, to be sure, circumstances involving national peril in which certain facts, far from being explained with candor, must be withheld from the public lest the enemy also learn them. The decision to withhold facts, in a democracy, is a grave one; and the action is not to be undertaken lightly. The key is correct judgment as to what few facts not already known to the enemy have such extraordinary importance, not how palatable they are for the public.

Censorship—that is, negative propaganda or withholding of dangerous secrets—can be permitted to a degree by a democracy in times of national peril. Propaganda based on lies, however, can never be justified. No government based on rule by the people can endure if it permits lying, for the reason that a deceived people —who are the source of government—cannot knowledgeably control their elected representatives. By their nature, lies by governing officials in a democracy are expressions of treason against that form of government, which depends on an informed electorate. The security of a nation may require silence in grievous emergencies; but the safety of a democracy cannot be more gravely endangered than by unchallenged lies.

To the degree that American propaganda has a false content, it will be self-defeating, in the long run, overseas, where contrary views can permeate and where skepticism concerning official propaganda, through centuries of exposure to its falsity, is prevalent; but at home such falsehood undermines the foundations of the Republic. Americans, who have governed themselves and have tended to trust their elected officials, are not yet conditioned to such skepticism; they may prefer to accept falsehoods rather than believe that their own representatives have lied to them. A democracy dare not permit betrayal of that trust; yet the tide of fantasy and falsehood is not receding in the United States—it may be that only an overwhelming force of public opinion can stop it even now. At home, however, America has the mechanisms to bring the pressure of opinion to bear; the problem, grave as it is, will be easier to solve than that of a falsely based foreign policy, on which uninformed or misinformed public opinion and scattered or occasional pressure groups, so far, have had no direct effect. Truth at home must be assured, first of all, to oblige truth overseas.

Perhaps as a first step toward a return to reality, Americans not already prisoners of fantasy might come together, as self-respecting individuals, in community groups modeled organizationally on our Better Business

103

Bureaus—groups which, with due investigation, would challenge fraudulent information practices. Here again American conservatives must in all probability play the key role; not because the conservative has any more understanding of the need for truth, but because the American liberal, ever since the fantasy era of the early 1950's, has been afraid to speak up for fear of being tarred with the "egghead" or "red" brush. The desperate need for truth to shed light on American policies, a need which involves national survival, should be great enough to bring together on this point both the liberal and the conservative wings of American thought. Transcending conservative and liberal differences is the common goal of preserving and defending the United States of America, which equals preservation and defense of the truth.

With reality once again shaping our perspectives at home, it would be far easier to evolve an effective propaganda based on the truth, in the great arena of conflict abroad, where the hearts and minds of men must be won or lost.

War is a serious game in which a man risks his reputation, his troops and his country.

— *Napoleon Bonaparte*

9

The Great "Little War"

As a new instrument of foreign-policy enforcement, designed specifically to counter the folk war and other upheaval-area risings, United States policy-makers decided to give special emphasis to a streamlined and attractively packaged form of "limited war," which came to be known popularly as the "little war." In 1961 a special-warfare unit was set up to handle an expected variety of unconventional military undertakings, particularly a variety called "guerrilla operations." The unit, despite its presumed "unconventional" nature and somewhat romanticized purpose, was not cloak-and-daggerish as was its predecessor "unitling" in the CIA; it was a more or less open organization, although not all its activities were for exhibit to casual passers-by.

The purpose of the new unit was to train "special forces" to work in the upheaval areas and counteract "subversion and guerrilla harassments against established governments," a phrase which, as we have seen, is a partial description of the folk war.

The same office in the Department of Defense that handled military aid for foreign countries, under Paul H. Nitze, assistant secretary of Defense for International Security Affairs, governed the unit, which also had close liaison with the Office of Research and Development, under the Secretary of Defense and its new section created by combining its tactical weapons and naval weapons research sections.

The idea, it was explained, was "to give the Reds a dose of their own oft-successful tactics of unconventional war—guerrilla harassment, sabotage and subversion—while avoiding the greater risks involved in conventional military operations." Troops would come from the upheaval areas themselves, principally from refugees, leavened by American technicians. Such tactics, it was asserted, could put the "Communists" on the defensive and "make it tougher for them to nibble away at free-world frontiers."

Around the world many thousands of tanned and tough young Americans, Asians, Latin Americans, Africans and refugee Europeans had for some time been busily learning to fight "unconventional wars" as a means of counteracting the folk wars, which of course, are also unconventional. The new emphasis came principally from General Maxwell Taylor, the first American officer of any standing to recognize that a nuclear stalemate had come into being and that a whole new concept might be needed. It was pushed to official acceptance by Taylor and by Lt. Gen. Arthur G. Trudeau, the Army's research and development officer.

Trudeau circulated a memorandum among senior military offices calling for an "all-out little war" that would even penetrate the borders of the Soviet Union and China. The memorandum proposed that the United States go beyond "mere" attack on the folk war. "We must find a way to overthrow communist regimes in power, short of a general war and even short of limited war," Trudeau wrote. "If they can afford a million dollars a year on propaganda alone in Latin America, and support a communist government in our back-yard, we can support free governments in Eastern Europe or any other area dominated by communists. Why should we fear general war in providing assistance to freedom fighters in Eastern Europe? The people are on our side there."

General Trudeau's memorandum, which contained much fancy and some logic, had momentary appeal after the Cuban fiasco, the "Little War" rehearsal. It served principally, however, not to initiate "little wars" against the Soviet Union, which would endanger the stalemate, under existing conditions, but to crystalize the policy of "fighting fire with fire." A "gray area" of warfare was defined, embracing guerrilla and counter-guerrilla activities, special intelligence operations and concentrated propaganda undertakings "to win over" the people in the folk-war areas. In working out this program, General Trudeau was left out in the cold. A special "task group" was put to work on a "secret" study, including, as usual, Attorney General Bob Kennedy,

General Taylor, and Admiral Arleigh Burke, Chief of Naval Operations at the time.

Unconventional warfare is hardly new; it has long been a thorn in the side of professional war chieftains, who have had an almost instinctive horror of it. Classically, it has been outlawed. In the First World War, before the value of *Schrecklichkeit* propaganda was understood, German regulars put to death thousands of French franc-tireurs without a single protest from the French high command, which looked with equal revulsion upon such breaches of formalism. The Geneva Convention, which set rules for "gentlemanly" warfare, provided no protection for patriots out of uniform who might take pot shots at the invading enemy. It was mutually agreed that killing was for uniformed men under conventional command.

Why, then, were Pentagon strategists, traditional military men to the core, training thousands of young men in techniques which violated the accepted rules? Why should the greatest military power on earth, splendidly equipped with conventional weapons, train an elite corps of its troops and assorted "refugees" in types of combat which, on the surface, resembled those of the Red Indians described by James Fenimore Cooper? The generals replied that the objective was to "put out brush fires" by fighting "fire with fire." They pointed with a mixture of resentment and puzzlement to "brush fires" such as Laos or Cuba or Algeria or Vietnam, as past or present examples. The "Red-led" peasants in such areas use all sorts of tricks which do not fit within the conventional rules; therefore we must use unconventional tactics against them.

The answer contained a grain of truth and logic;

but it skirted the main issue. Brush fires, conventional or unconventional, are nothing new. For generations there have been "Fuzzy-wuzzy" risings in Africa, Sandino actions in Latin America, Philippine insurrections, Boxer Rebellions and Pancho Villa raids. In all these "brush fires," unconventional tactics used by presumed nationalist peasants against presumed colonialist bearers of the white man's burden were answered by conventional means. Regular army or marine detachments were used in conventional, even routine ways to impose superiority in such risings. The Fuzzy-wuzzies broke British *squares*; the British squares, not anti-guerrillas or special forces, broke the Fuzzy-wuzzies. The British, who bore the burden of the West in those days, for the most part went about their task in workman-like fashion, with no excitement and no talk of "little wars."

Obviously, routine brush fires would not arouse the Pentagon or other NATO, CENTO or SEATO military centers to the degree of emphasis on unconventional warfare that was prescribed. It was plain that what was happening in the trouble centers of Asia, Latin America and Africa did not fit into any traditional brush-fire category. What the Pentagon was confronted with was the "poor man's atom bomb," the folk war. Raging according to plan, it turned the traditional brush fire into controlled forest fires. For the first time in history, unconventional warfare had developed a science of its own and at point of contact had nullified conventional opposition.

This is the realization that led the Pentagon to emphasize unconventional military preparation and to train picked forces in the techniques of the "little war." Itself unconventional in outward form, the "little war"

109

was seen as at least a stop-gap answer to the folk war. A confusion between form and substance seemed to have developed once again, however.

Although "little war" is a literal translation of *guerrilla* in Spanish, it is a translation of the word rather than the sense. Interchangeable use of the terms by the Pentagon indicated a degree of failure to understand the difference between unconventional operations, as envisaged for the "little war," and the whole realm of unconventional strategy that characterizes the folk war. A contrast between "little war" possibilities and one phase of the folk war, guerrilla operations, will illustrate a part of this difference:

The "little war," despite grandiose plans for "propaganda penetration," cannot possibly depend on popular support, that is, majority support, in any area of folk war, for the simple reason that a folk war is possible only when popular support for it, in an overwhelming majority, has already been mobilized. The folk war *is* the majority. Guerrilla operations, as part of the overall folk-war framework, cannot exist without popular support; the guerrillas *are* the people. In every important way, the "little war," in contrast, will have to depend on outside sustenance—arms, munitions, air cover, transport, command; yet guerrilla activities can succeed only to the degree they are not dependent on outside sustenance. The "little war" might be described as an unconventional finger attached to a conventional hand; guerrilla operations, as employed in the folk war, are an unconventional part fully integrated into and unseparable from an unconventional framework.

To maintain a "little war" and keep it from being

swallowed up in the hostile environment that itself generates the folk war, sizable conventional forces would have to be used effectively to control the sky above and the sea around the "little war" area and to rope off the equivalent of beachheads into which only carefully guarded natives or "refugees" would be allowed.

These factors may have been considered by the "little war" planners but they were obviously not fully understood. The same flaw was evident in their analysis that was evident also in the other arms of policy enforcement made use of by the United States in rigid adherence to doctrines originating with the foreign-investor pressure group. The "little war," once again, would work with the minority power elite, the "refugees" from the folk war; the folk war, in contrast, is based on the great submerged majority, the huge out-group coming to power.

In the discussions which preceded and accompanied the decision (basically President Kennedy's) to concentrate on limited or "little war," the main argument did not at any time reach the heart of the "people" issue. The argument was essentially that "if the United States does not have an effective limited-war force, backed by a program of economic, social and military reform, it will be faced with three unacceptable choices: Using its nuclear weapons (impossible in the present stalemate); resisting ineffectively, as in Laos; or not resisting at all." Thus, the argument ran, "the United States must either give emphasis to limited war or risk a series of piecemeal military and diplomatic defeats." What this argument boiled down to, it appeared, was that a limited war was better than none. The mention of "economic, social and military reform," as applied to upheaval areas, could not, unfortunately, be more than double-talk: The minority power elite in these areas, already wallowing in gifts from the United States, could hardly be expected to take steps which, in its view, would benefit their deadly enemy, their own people.

It is true, of course, that United States conventional military assistance to the existing governments in the upheaval areas has largely gone down the drain. In the cold-war period, up to the end of the 1960 fiscal year only, the United States had given these areas, in military equipment alone, the following amounts:

Aid in Military Equipment

	(millions)	
Afghanistan	$2	
Brazil	153	
Cambodia	68	
Chile	40	
Colombia	26	
Cuba	11	(Batista regime)
Dominican Republic	7	(Trujillo)
Ecuador	18	
Formosa	2,550	
Guatemala	2+	
Haiti	6	
Honduras	1.2	
Iran	460	(following CIA *coup d'etat*)
Iraq	50	(prior to uprising)
Jordan	20	
Lebanon	10	
Laos	70	(not incl. $300 million during later crisis)
Mexico	5	

	(millions)	
Nicaragua	$2	
Paraguay	1	
Peru	52	
Philippines	355	
Portugal	300	
Spain	500+	
Thailand	354	
Turkey	2,100	
Uruguay	24	
Venezuela	40	
Vietnam	1,210	(incl. aid during 1953)

Counted in these values, for the Latin American countries, was the cost (including surplus valuations) only for tanks, trucks, aircraft, anti-aircraft weapons and electronic equipment, nothing else; in the Far East total there were aircraft, machine guns, war vessels, trucks, bulldozers and tanks; and in the Near East, the total was limited to tanks, aircraft, small arms, ammunition and minesweepers. For the presumed upheaval areas, in this class of equipment, this came to around $11,200 million. Africa, not of deep concern until after the 1960 fiscal year, absorbed only some $60 million, most of it going to Ethiopia. The total sum spent in this way, despite a somewhat cheaper selection of equipment, was not far below the amount spent on Europe from 1945 through June 1960, which was $14,830 million. Formosa, incidentally, obtained twice as much military aid in this form as did Great Britain.

These expenditures in the upheaval lands, repeatedly proved futile in conditions of folk war, could, it was argued, have built up swift, efficient "limited war" forces that could have put a stop to "Red" penetration.

113

The "little war," it was thought, would be cheaper. Using similar economic reason, one might argue that it would be far, far cheaper, as Chapter 11 will indicate, simply to help the people of the upheaval areas decide their own forms of government, for the United States to go with the tide rather than against it. If the Soviet Union or China, run by minority dictatorships, can appear to take the side of the majority groups in the upheaval lands, it would seem feasible for the United States, run at least by pressure groups probably totaling a majority, to take the majority side in fact. Not only would such a step save billions now wasted; it would also save the need for so much argument about the values of a "limited war." The folk wars are already underway; why not help them win and save money as well as friends—and stop the Soviet Union and China at the same time?

However, rather than go to the touchy heart of the matter, which involves, as all foreign policy problems do for the United States, the basic snag of the alliance between declining minority power centers and American overseas investors, the "little war" technicians concentrated on romanticized or technical aspects. Their vocabulary was replete with such terms as "fast-moving specialized detachments, well-equipped with light weapons," "destruction of power centers," "sabotage of communications," "the fight for freedom."

Penetration of folk-war territories would be undertaken in secret border crossings, nighttime parachute drops in isolated areas and in small coastal landings, with regrouping of the small bodies of fierce guerrillas at designated areas for attack. Sudden but relatively open invasion with larger bodies of specialized troops was also discussed, to be undertaken in theoretical areas where "heavy support" among dissident elements of the population could be counted on. Emphasis was placed on recruitment and training of nationals of proposed target areas of the "little war," selected from among "refugees." Americans, who would of course hold positions of command and of technical responsibility, were taught local languages and customs for the purpose. In ideal circumstances, it was theorized, the "little war" could be disguised as a spontaneous reply by native patriots to the tyranny of Communist usurpers, with the use of slogans such as "bread," "land," "freedom" and the like, every bit as profusely as the folk warriors themselves. There would be preparation for both offensive and defensive operations. The "little war" would be employed to overthrow a hostile regime or to defend a friendly one.

These theories and objectives, however, were hard to square with the essential nature of the "little war" as a military undertaking. In fact, as opposed to grandiose theory, it differs little from the commando raids, espionage drops and sabotage undertakings made by the Allies in the war against the Axis. These raids had many small successes, although, in retrospect, their importance to the course of war seems less now than it did then; but even in this respect the sponsors of the "little war" have overlooked an essential difference in conditions. Much of the territory occupied by the Axis was inhabited by populations engaged in passive or active resistance to occupation authorities, who were German, Japanese or other Axis foreigners; in sharp contrast, the populations in areas that would be "little war" targets would in the great majority be hostile to intruders.

115

Moreover, they would be organized, in the folk-war manner, for precisely the type of "invasion" that the "little war" envisages; such attacks are presumed in folk-war strategy, since it takes into account the alliance between the minority power group, on the national level, and the internationally based investor group.

Two attempts at "little war" rehearsals in early 1961 illustrated how techniques that had value for commando raids, with limited objectives, were naïvely ineffective when used under conditions of popular hostility. These were the attack on Cuba, whose planning was carried out precisely by those most imbued with the "little war" theory, and the air-drops of "guerrillas" behind the Pathet Lao lines in Laos. Both these operations demonstrated that the "little war" concept, as it now stands, is valueless without massive support from conventional forces. Yet conventional forces could not possibly have been used, because of the overriding danger of a U. S.-Soviet or U. S.-Chinese clash and because of the obvious repercussions on Latin American or Asian public opinion. It would seem that the "little war" idea will have limited value as an answer to the genuine folk war; it cannot stand by itself, while the folk war can, in all its forms.

The argument for preparation of "little wars" is, in itself, not unpersuasive. It is based mainly on the belief that "paramilitary" warfare would in fact be less deadly than any other available form of warfare, and that it would be safer, because of its presumably concealed origin—it would save face for the Soviets, who would not be obliged to rattle their rockets in reply. Some sort of war, it is argued, is the only way of preventing the "Communists" from taking over the whole world; and, of all available forms, the "little war" would be the best in the circumstances. The flaw in this argument lies in its premise that the military danger is "communism." This sounds like a vote-catching politician's attitude, not that of a military man; because any military man should immediately and almost intuitively know that the only military danger the United States confronts at present comes from the Soviet Union, with its Chinese ally, the only military power strong enough to face us. The "Communists" are not a military menace; they are a menace on the people level; they penetrate existing majority movements against minority cliques in alliance with our foreign investors.

Frequently, the clash between the majority group and the minority clique will take a military form; but the issue at this point is rarely communism, it is what old-fashioned Americans called "democracy." The point of conflict between the national interests of the United States and those of the Soviet Union is not in the clash between the minority power clique and the national majority; it is in the jockeying for control between the leaders of the national majority and the Communist penetrators, which normally comes as or *after* the majority wins out over the minority clique. It is the failure to understand this fact, by American policy-makers blinded by pressures from our overseas investors acting strictly in their short-range and presumed *private* interests, which has created our problems in this field. Intervention, by "little war" or otherwise, on the side of the dictatorial minority and against the essentially democratic majority (a majority is the only basis for democracy, which means rule by the people), produces an automatic reaction in favor of the "Communists," on the

117

people level and, therefore, in favor of the Soviet Union. We are, in this respect, our own most powerful enemy.

Our essential failure, therefore, in considering the "little war" as an answer to the folk war, comes from not analyzing the real problem. If we had, without bias, we would have discovered that the folk war is not only "the poor man's atom bomb"; it is a remarkable offensive and defensive *majority* weapon used to overthrow dictatorial minority groups; against it any known kind of military action, short of genocide, will fail in the long run. The "secret arm" is people, organized and hard-fighting majorities. Against people, only people can be finally effective.

As an instrument of foreign policy enforcement, the "little war" comes up against the same barrier to effective action as have our intelligence and propaganda services: A basic flaw in our foreign policy itself, the fact that it is aimed at serving the interests of American overseas investors and not the over-all national interests of the United States. To be successful, at this phase of conflict with the Soviet Union, in a period of military stalemate, in the use of any instrument of foreign policy, we have to go with the tide of people, not against it; otherwise we blunt our own weapons and turn over the balance of power—people—to the Soviet Union. Let us examine possible causes and cures of this problem.

PART 3

SUGGESTIONS AND CASES

t is not the Communists who made these areas inflammable. Rather, it is the ideas and achievements of Western man, who carried Western civilization into every nook and cranny of the globe.

— *Eugene R. Black*

Commencement Address, University of Hartford, June 11, 1961.

10

American Dilemma

As we shall see in Chapter 14, the dilemma in policy enforcement the United States faces does not arise from the military stand-off with the Soviet Union. The American dilemma comes, rather, from the Soviet breakthrough on the "people front," as described. The breakthrough, however, was our own fault; it was not achieved by the Soviet Union through diabolical cleverness; it was given to them by American policy-makers on the proverbial silver platter.

Although defeat on the people front would weaken the United States and lead to increasing loss of prestige,

121

it would probably not lead soon to outright decline of
the United States as a military power and consequent
military defeat at the hands of the Soviet Union. The
effect would tend to be one of retreat rather than out
right defeat; loss of our remaining allies among the
world's peoples, and the inevitable elimination of the
parasitic ruling minorities in the upheaval areas, would
thrust the United States back into a "Fortress America"
behind nuclear walls. It would imply, probably, dicta
torship at home. Isolated, perhaps quarantined, we
should in fact have nothing left to fight for; and internal
collapse would finally open the gates.

Defeat on the people front is, however, unneces
sary; it is not a fated thing, in the hands of the gods.
it comes, it will be a product of our own failure to take
honest and logical action. Just why American foreign
policy has so insistently taken the opposite side to the
popular upheavals and folk wars that are a main cha
acteristic of this period in history may seem an in
explicable mystery to the casual observer. American
traditions, its great colonial revolution, the war (at leas
in part) against slavery and our innumerable pro-people
word symbols—which still mean what they say to the
submerged majorities—all these intensify the myster
and wrap it in an enigma which, for most of the world
has become more enigmatic than that of the Soviet
described by Winston Churchill.

On close examination—if preconceptions are le
aside—the mystery dissipates. The key to understanding
lies in the nature of the process by which American
foreign policy is formed. This process is quite different
from that which produces domestic policies; domestic
policy, or politics, is a product of checks and balances

It results from the interplay of the three independent branches of government and a variety of pressure groups, in or out of political parties. For the most part, according to the degrees of pressures exerted, domestic policy represents a fusion of many interests. Foreign policy, in sharp contrast, overrides most of this complicated machinery. Subject to only minor checks, it is the province of the Executive branch of the American government, as provided by the Constitution, whose framers saw the need for fast, unhampered action in foreign affairs. Instead of the multitudinous checks, balances and pressure groups that participate in the formation of domestic policy, there is only one major pressure group that can bring its force to bear on the foreign policy of the United States. This pressure group, obviously, is international American business; there is no counteracting force except, in rare instances, a sudden and temporary awakening of sections of public opinion, an awakening often brought on by international American business, through public relations techniques, to provide additional leverage for a particular point of policy.

In these circumstances, it is only natural that more often than not American foreign policy is determined, not by the pressures which determine domestic policies, but by the single effective pressure group concerned. These private interests are the only day-by-day interests America has overseas; from this standpoint, the heavy influence they bring to bear on American foreign policy may be justified, in normal times. American investments have in many cases contributed substantially to the material well-being of underdeveloped areas, providing also, on the average, higher returns for stockholders than could be expected from investments at home.

There is a general and understandable tendency for American national interests overseas to be identified with the private interests of American overseas investors. In terms of policy formation in the interests of the American people as a whole, particularly in times when national survival may be at stake, this identification is a mixed blessing. National interests, at such times, will encompass much more than the protection or expansion of investments.

The United States is now in such a period, by far the most critical for national survival since the War between the States; a period more critical for survival of traditional American institutions has, indeed, never been known. In such periods it is conceivable that limited interests must at times be sacrificed for the greater goal of national interest, if no other solution is at hand.

It has been observed that it was American investments, along with others from the industrialized West, which, from economic necessity, organized the out-group majorities in the underdeveloped countries for the first time. American and other investors organized the underdeveloped world economically to provide raw materials for smelters and mills at home; then gradually, they began to build their factories at the site of production, increasing the degree of economic organization.

Colonialism, economic and political, has been excoriated; but the pre-colonial lands were not idyllic paradises where dusky inhabitants lolled beneath coconut trees, ambling now and then into green groves to pluck a ripe banana or make love. They were lands infested with disease, filth, parasitic worms, mosquitoes dysentery, and where periodic massacres occurred. So

124

cial organization was simple; the chief or king or dictator was boss; his subjects obeyed him or were knocked
over the head. There were no organized revolts; no folk
wars. Without organization there was no mechanism for
revolt. Weapons were primitive, communications poor.

Businessmen from the industrial West moved into
these lands. The spirit of efficiency was instilled, drilled
or beaten into the inhabitants. Time, other than meal-
time, nighttime or daytime, began to have meaning.
The vast out-groups, brought together to dig minerals,
harvest cocoa or rubber or to work in the new factories,
came to know each other; they worked together; they
communicated. In short, they were organized. Out of
this organization there arose the basis for social and
political—and military—organization, without which the
present upheaval of the submerged majorities in the
underdeveloped lands would be formless and ineffective.

The investments from the industrial West also
obliged alliances and understandings between the investors and the local power elite. On the earliest level,
no more was needed than a gift to a chieftain, in return
for which he supplied his subjects for cheap labor. On
the modern level, the relationship between the governing power elite in the upheaval areas and the investor
takes on more of the nature of a symbiosis: The power
elite cannot survive without support from the international investors, who may, and frequently do, become
the dominant partner in the alliance. On the other hand,
the need for a guarantee of investment security and
adequate return obliges the investor to maintain the
power elite in control, or, at most, to shift from one
minority ruling group to another in *coups d'etat*. The
need to maintain this alliance has automatically aligned

American investors against the rising out-group majorities in every underdeveloped country.

It is this alignment, the product of economic circumstance, which has created the dilemma for American foreign policy. America has been faced with the choice of either going against the immediate economic interests of its overseas investors in the upheaval lands, with many billions of dollars at stake, or of going against the overwhelming tide of change represented by the rebelling majorities. The choice had, of course, always existed; but until the present era it did not present a dilemma. American overseas investors, in their obvious interests, shored up the power elite in each underdeveloped land in which they had economic objectives; American foreign policy went along with them—into Mexico, Nicaragua, Cuba, Haiti, Panama, the Phillippines and so on, in an earlier era, into the wide world in the great investment expansion that followed World War II. No national danger, except, from time to time, to the national sense of right and wrong, was involved in the decision to use foreign policy to back up American nationals with overseas interests. It was assumed that the American flag followed them.

The dilemma arose with the entry of the Soviet Union on the world scene, after decades of isolation, and the growing power of its new Chinese ally. Soviet commercial and financial dealings were carried out by the Soviet government itself; no private investors, no private interests, were involved. There was no split, in the case of the Soviet Union, between private and national interest; they were one and the same. The Soviet Union thus had a free hand to give or withhold economic support for any group in the underdeveloped nations; and it shrewdly avoided getting tied up, even on temporary bases, with the weakening power elite. It employed its economic resources, even its international trade, as a lever to throw the balance toward one group or another. Economic intercourse was at all times subject to government control and to manipulation in line with Soviet foreign policy.

In this way, the Soviet Union was free to align itself with whichever side in the underdeveloped area appeared to be on the upswing, in power or soon to come to power. Unlike the United States, the Soviet Union was always in position, at any given time, to swing its support in any direction determined by its national interests. As the great upheavals took place, as the majority out-groups in the developing lands rose, the Soviet Union could join them; it had no vested interest in maintaining the declining power elite. It was thus able to make full use of the "people base" to throw the United States off balance.

Obliged to protect its investors and their properties in close alliance with the minority ruling groups in the upheaval areas, the United States was pinned down to a single position. Regardless of the course that history was taking, regardless of the instinctive sympathy that most Americans felt for the rising masses of people and their disgust for the corrupt overlords at last being overthrown, the United States, imprisoned by economic ties, was obliged to buck the tide. Automatically, America was aligned on the side of status quo; automatically also, we lost, and continue to lose, in each area of the world where the status quo is faced with the irresistible onrush of change. We lose, repeatedly, because we are on the losing side. Contrary to our Jeffersonian principles, we fight majority rule.

The freedom of movement of the Soviet Union in the upheaval areas, as contrasted with the enforced immobility of the United States, goes far to explain why, in those areas—contrary to what Americans have been told—the Soviet Union has come to be regarded as the natural ally of popular movements and the natural foe of corrupt dictatorships. The fine, anticolonial words of the United States fall flat in the upheaval lands against the concrete facts of Soviet anticolonial action. The same freedom of movement explains why, in the United Nations, the Soviet Union has been able to assume the somewhat awkward role of defender of all exploited underdogs against "imperialist piracy," while the United States, despite the billions of dollars in outright gifts poured into backward regions, finds itself pushed into corners as the principal imperialist pirate.

Because of its immobile role as the mainstay of the power elite and the dictatorships, a role assumed because of the pressure brought to bear on American policy by our overseas investors, America's "moral" position has degenerated not only in the underdeveloped areas but around the world. We are maneuvered into actions that can have no moral justification, however great the economic cause. America has a tiger or possibly a polecat by the tail; the problem is how to let go without at the same time letting go of countless billions of dollars invested by American business overseas. An unchallenged world power, as America imagined itself to be after World War II, can afford a few moral lapses; the great empires of the past hardly set records for righteousness. But in a polarized world of stalemate between two awesomely potent powers, every featherweight on the balance counts. Quite simply, America cannot afford to lose; defeat means the end. We must have the people of the world on our side, otherwise the balance of power will inevitably go against us.

Let us emphasize the fact again: The Soviet Union has freedom of movement; it can provide or withdraw support anywhere at any time because it has only its national interests to consider. The United States in contrast is immobilized because its foreign policy veers, not in line with its over-all national interest, but according to the degree of pressure exerted by special group interest. Because these private interests, wherever they have set up shop in the underdeveloped areas, have been obliged by economic circumstance to ally themselves with the minority group in power, they are automatically opposed to the incoming tide of majority upheaval. So long as the United States is guided by these private interests and not by the interest of the nation as a whole, our foreign policy will likewise move against the tide and we will suffer continual and ultimate defeat.

Hard though the choice may be, the United States will sooner or later have to formulate its foreign policy on the basis of national interest if it is to survive—and since the survival of American international business is directly tied to survival of the United States, it should be possible to work out a practical solution once the urgent need for a solution is understood. So far, however, the United States has continued with the old method of forming foreign policy. Around the world our forces are mobilized to strike against the tides of upheaval and against the folk wars. It is possible that some American policy-makers, rather than make what appears to be a choice between the devil and the deep blue sea, prefer to throw the full weight of the United States against the gigantic onrush of this human flood, in the hope that new conditions will be created, new circumstances of choice. A gamble of this sort, with the very future of the nation at stake, hardly qualifies even as a calculated risk. It is mere stupidity. And it is also unnecessary.

It is possible to find a way to cut American policy loose from its bonds and give full mobility to outmaneuver the Soviet Union in the use of people power. It is possible to do this with a bold move which would avoid fatal losses for American overseas investors and at the same time win friends and influence people in the upheaval areas, leaving the Soviet Union without its principal weapon.

Let us examine this potential before placing our hands over our eyes and jumping off into the unknown. We do not need to be anti-people or oppose our own Jeffersonian principles.

At times I am aghast to think
what will happen when we really
get started with the advance
guard of coca-cola, chewing gum
and guns.

— Rev. Theodore M. Hesburgh

Talk, Columbia University
Alumni Federation, June 6, 1961.

11

Mobility in Foreign Policy

In theory, foreign policy is derived through careful
analysis, through definition of national interest in each
case, study and interpretation of facts in the area of application, and choice of the means of putting the policy
into effect. If national interest is not defined, there is
no point in having a policy. If the facts are not known,
there is no way to judge whether or not the policy is
correct. And if the wrong means of policy enforcement
have been chosen, then even the best policy and the
most thorough knowledge would mean nothing. Study

131

of each case implies that foreign policy must be mobile, because each case in which it is to be applied will vary.

American foreign policy has apparently been formed, however, on the basis of some other theory: We have failed to define our policy in terms of national interest, because of the pressures of a private group, and we have been boxed into a fixed position, lost mobility, because of the same pressures. This has led us into the worst policy debacle in our history, blinded us to facts and their nature as a policy basis, and has so increased the odds against us that effective means of policy enforcement can no longer be applied; we are immobilized. In the interest of national survival, the United States must consider how to cut the restraining bonds that have held us in fixed and futile postures while the Soviet Union, with inferior resources, has been free to dash in and out, jabbing at every weak point.

We must start from the premise that, after all, there is nothing sacrosanct about some Americans' overseas business, and that there is something sacrosanct about the United States of America. This is not a new premise, although it is rarely mentioned; any high-school boy will, if need be, fight and die for his country; but not even the most dyed-in-the-wool "corporation man" will feel a patriotic thrill at the sight of his company's name plate. We may even presume that if, at some future date, a clear choice were to arise between sacrificing all the billions various groups of Americans have invested overseas and endangering the survival of America itself, then not even the most callous chairman of the board would oppose that sacrifice. Fortunately, that is not the choice America must make today to defeat the Soviet Union in the use of people power. It should, however, be clear that America's over-all foreign policy should not, and cannot in present critical circumstances, be the same as that of its overseas investors nor be dictated by them. No single pressure group, however important, should be allowed to prescribe the foreign policy of the people of the United States at any time, and especially not in a time of crisis.

Working quite understandably on behalf of its special interests, which it has a right to do, American overseas business, as described, pressured the United States to come to its aid and to the aid of the minority ruling groups, allied to it, which have come under fire by the majorities as they rise. So far, the United States has yielded to this pressure, since no contrary pressure in the over-all national interest has been exerted. That is why, in conditions of nuclear stalemate and in the face of a frequent counterbalancing alliance between the rising majorities and the Soviet Union, the United States has been blocked and defeated with monotonous regularity. Its policy has many times forced the rising majorities, in their battle with the "investor-minority symbiosis," to seek out on their own initiative the balancing aid of the Soviet Union or China, which is only too available. Thus, on the most critical of all fronts, the United States has lost more even than is visible; and the Soviet Union, maneuvering with complete mobility against our unvarying position, has been the propaganda victor even when the rising majorities, as in cases such as Guinea, Indonesia or Algeria, have been able to fend off Soviet control.

There is no logical reason why, if the United States could free itself from its enforced alliance with minority cliques and petty dictatorships, it could not rapidly eliminate the Soviet Union as a major influence in the underdeveloped areas, making use of its infinitely greater resources.

The problem, therefore, is how to free our hands, turn about, and help the rising majorities achieve their modicum of democracy, to be ourselves, not bodyguards for gangsters, and yet not sacrifice our investors unnecessarily. The overseas investors themselves have come up with what may be one answer. They have asked (among the "they" are such representatives as Stanley de J. Osborne, president of Olin Mathieson Chemical Corporation, F. Taylor Ostrander of American Metal Climax and Chad F. Calhoun of Kaiser Industry) for "investment insurance," guaranteed by the government of the United States, against "all but business risks and our own stupidity." A significant and concrete proposal along these lines was made by Harold S. Geneen, president of International Telephone & Telegraph Corp., which may indicate the growth of this new trend among American overseas business. In consultations with Senator Smathers of Florida, considered an effective spokesman for such interests and a key member of the Senate Foreign Commerce Committee, Geneen observed frankly that his company was prepared to invest $250 million in Latin American operations between 1962 and 1967 alone—if the United States government would insure the investments against political loss and upheavals. Establishment of such guarantees would be necessary "to restore the confidence" of the investors, he declared.

What this means, plainly, is that American overseas investors are ready and willing to participate in government insurance programs that would guard against the possibility of expropriation of properties by the incoming governments of the rising majorities. In fact, foreign-aid agencies of the United States already have authority to insure American investments abroad, although the authority has been little used. Newly strengthened guarantees, offering broad political protection to private American enterprises, have been written into these insurance measures. With some further strengthening, the measures could assure investors that they would at least get their money back if the upheaval leaders, striking at their enemies, take over the investors' properties.

Entry into such an insurance scheme by major American investors overseas could serve at least three essential purposes: First, and probably most important, acceptance by investors of insurance against "political risk" would give the United States government, for the first time, a means of control over any possible political adventuring by American corporations overseas. Political activities by such corporations which might incur a risk of reprisal would border on fraudulent practice; and a definition to that effect in the insurance terms would caution investors to consider penalties before giving support to local dictatorships or other minority regimes. The United States could thus avoid being linked, through investor ties, with political machinations either for or against local regimes. Above all, it would have an understandable means of enforcing a "hands off" policy among international investor groups. Second, an insurance plan of this sort could be interpreted to guarantee individual American stockholders against monetary loss. With such a guarantee, they would tend to view much more dispassionately and logically the inevitable majority take-over in the upheaval areas.

(It is probable that a sharp division should be made in such plans between reimbursement of American stockholders and others. It is sometimes forgotten that "American" corporations overseas are, in many cases, neither American in name nor in ownership. A substantial minority of stock will usually be held by nationals of the investment area, representing the local power elite; the corporation itself will be registered and incorporated under the laws of the country it enters; and stockholders even in the home corporation, which normally controls a majority of stock in the subsidiary, will include a substantial percentage of non-Americans. Overseas subsidiaries are headless offshoots of headless parents; as in all large American corporations, there are no real owners, only managers and stockholders. In some countries—Mexico for example—a majority of stock must be held by nationals; how can such a company be called American? And why should the United States be obliged to guard the interests of non-Americans?)

Third, as a benefit from the insurance scheme, the United States would be in position, in cases where the interests of its citizens were definitely involved, to negotiate as a government with the expropriating government concerning reimbursement of losses incurred by American *citizens*. It could offer easy repayment terms, even loan funds with which to make repayment, or accept payment in local currency, which the United States now does in selling surplus foodstuffs, for example.

If such a plan had been in force in the case of Cuba, at the time of the Castro take-over, the United States would have had sufficient mobility, if national interest had so determined, to have reached a facile understanding with the new regime—which, after all, offered repayment of expropriations on terms not unlike those arranged by the United States in Japan following the expropriations caused by the MacArthur reforms. The total value of properties, installations and liquid assets held in Cuba by nominally American subsidiaries was around $1,200 million, although not all was on the tax books. Total losses to the United States, through private and government reprisal actions on both sides, military, propaganda and CIA expenditures, export-market loss, import-profit loss, elimination of interest and profit remittances and dividends (and the sums rushed frantically to Latin America as anti-Cuban buffers) would certainly total far more than the expropriations—which were, to a degree, written off as tax losses by the American corporations concerned. In effect, in Cuba, we cut off our nose to spite our face.

In a different kind of case, where intelligent action is still possible, as in Thailand, we have so far been equally unbusiness-like as well as unwise in policies. In Thailand, through 1960, we had spent well over $250 million in "economic aid" and $300 million in "military equipment" to bolster our alliance with a minority regime of doubtful longevity; yet our total private investment there, so far as can be determined among the maze of peculiar arithmetic, could not have been more than 20 per cent of that $550 million total. There, if anywhere on earth, we should have been able to keep free of an entangling alliance, free to take sides with the majority if need be and to join with them in preventing any Chinese or Soviet encroachment. Certainly, insurance of our investments, and payment for their expropriation if necessary, would in almost every case tend to be cheaper than our present methods and, above all, would enable us to move with the majority side—indeed, with any force we might choose in specific conditions.

Still another advantage which an adequate insurance scheme would make possible would be to encourage American investors, in full awareness of circumstances, to enter new nations, products of upheaval, such as those now developing in Africa, on the terms they offer. A friendly, nonpolitical, non-pressure relationship between constructive American investors and the new African regimes, with neither side fearful of the future and with full recognition on both sides of the sovereign right of expropriation, could be helpful in turning those governments toward the United States rather than slowly against us, as now. Insurance schemes should, of course, be considered more or less stop-gap measures, applicable as problems arise, with the objective of giving the United States a freer hand for policy maneuvers.

A second factor, probably of even greater significance, which may eventually enable American policymakers to cut the bonds that hold them now, is the development of a rather new form of overseas enterprise. This is the trend, apparent also in the United States itself, toward service capital. There are major American enterprises, with operations around the world, which build factories or pipelines or provide skilled engineers or managers strictly as a service. Once the facilities are built and functioning, ownership abides with the foreign government or locally owned enterprise which ordered the service. The American service company pockets its profit, usually substantial, and moves on to another assignment. If the local government changes hands or if the rising majority sweeps to power, the problem of ownership remains strictly domestic; the United States would not have to take sides, as it does under present conditions of pressure when so-called American property interests are involved. American corporations engaged in this type of endeavor, such as Fish International, for example, have consistently recorded higher profit percentages than those insisting on the ownership principle—with no long-term risk of expropriation and no need for a continuing, ever more strangling alliance with minority cliques.

The National Construction Association, with twenty-eight engineering and building contractors as members, reported that they are working on more than two hundred overseas service undertakings, ranging from giant industrial complexes to construction of electric substations. Stone & Webster Engineering Corp. of Boston said its own staff engineers are often working in a score of countries. In 1960, these engineers traveled 665,000 miles on service jobs abroad. The Construction Industry International Committee, with more than sixty members, estimated that just seventeen of those members completed upward of $2,500 million worth of projects overseas in five years up to 1961, generating demand for upward of a billion dollars in U.S. machinery and equipment. It is not improbable that these and other American service firms, counting profits retained at the point of operation, re-invested overseas in new enterprises, remitted to tax havens and returned to the United States, are netting already, in this early phase, more than a billion dollars a year. A decade ago, except for government-contracted work on overseas military installations, this type of service work was considered unusual.

Enterprises such as these could easily work in harmony with the incoming majority groups, once they take power. The leaders of the new wave of popular government in the upheaval lands are economically conscious; they are aware of the need for vast expansion of productive facilities, for installation of processing equipment, construction of new transportation, the thousand and one requirements for higher living standards neglected by the minority dictatorships which sought only benefits for themselves and based their economies, frequently, on monoculture. Cuba exported up to six million tons of sugar a year while its people starved for fresh foods that had to be imported. Throughout the underdeveloped world the phenomenon of undernourishment exists side by side with burgeoning production of raw materials—rubber, cocoa, coffee, tin, copper and so on—produced for consumption elsewhere. The incoming popular governments will have to start production for their people almost from scratch; a tremendous and profitable field exists there for American engineering and service companies, for builders rather than exploiters.

The Soviet Union has already observed the danger of this American trend; perhaps overestimating the official acumen of the United States, it has rushed its own "service companies" to the scene, building Egypt's dam, constructing steel mills in India, planning oil refineries in Indonesia, sending crowds of technicians into each new land of strategic value. Yet, in each case, the Soviet Union has taken great care not to "own" anything; it sells, loans or "gives" its services and construction, avoiding permanent commitment on a political

140

level and any need for a symbiotic alliance that would tie its hands.

Many circumstances indicate that the day of "foreign" investment, for ownership purposes, is rapidly drawing to a close; however, it will not end soon enough to give automatic freedom to the United States in formation of foreign policy in this crisis period. It is probable that the United States should hasten this trend, meanwhile softening its effect on genuine American investors by schemes such as that now possible for insurance against expropriation. Foreign investment, implying ownership of properties in one country by nationals of another, served the historic purpose of organizing, for production and for eventual political action, the great submerged majorities in the underdeveloped world. This was not the conscious purpose of the foreign investors; but it was their historic purpose, which has now been fulfilled in much of the world. The new trend is toward both economic and political independence among the rising nations in Latin America, Asia and Africa; economic dependence, the characteristic given these countries in the past by foreign ownership of their economies, implied political dependence; economic independence, the present goal, likewise implies political independence. The role of foreign capital in the upheaval areas must now, of necessity, in view of the decline from power of manipulable minorities, be subservient, no longer one of control.

One way in which the United States can hasten the natural decline of "ownership" capital and speed the development of "service" capital, thus freeing itself from the no longer bearable pressure of its foreign investors, would be to recognize the obvious fact, already

141

indicated, that most presumably American "ownership" capital invested overseas is either not in fact American or at most is expatriate. Corporations, legally, are persons, subjected to the same obligations. If an American takes citizenship in a foreign country, he is no longer eligible for the protection of the United States but is thenceforth bound by the laws of his adopted country. Whatever that country may do for him or to him is no longer the affair of the United States. The same rule applies to corporations, regardless of the source of capital that formed them. The United States has no obligations of any kind toward expatriate American capital which has entered into corporations that are "citizens" of a foreign country; it has assumed these obligations, *extralegally*, because of the pressures of American investors of capital. Simple recognition, in official American policy, of this legal fact would do more to free our foreign policy from its present rigidity than any other measure now available. At the same time, such recognition would hasten the decline of "ownership" capital and give impetus to "service" capital, which has taken over the role of historic purpose, of furthering the principle of majority control.

It is plain that the United States does not have to choose between the devil and the deep blue sea in its effort to build a mobile foreign policy that can counteract Soviet maneuvers. All the policy-makers have to do, admittedly easier said, is to plan and act in accordance with national needs and let the foreign-investor pressure group adjust to reality. Expropriation insurance can help soften the blow; and a switch to the new field of "service" capital can eliminate much of the problem for worried investors. But it is, after all, their private problem; the basic problem of the American people is one of national survival, not the survival of a declining business group.

Perhaps we could begin trying out these possibilities in the upheaval area closest to us and most vital, strategically and economically, to our national interests—Latin America. For the first time in many years, American policy-makers have turned their attention southward, startled awake by Cuba and by a pronounced swing, in the key countries, toward "independentism." Latin America provides an opportunity for the United States to make "a clinical test" of a corrected policy. Unfortunately, the policy is still not available, except in vague palliative forms, as we shall observe in the next chapter.

Economic and social progress in many countries of Latin America will require radical, even revolutionary changes of some of the institutions.

— Comm. for Economic Development

Pamphlet, Cooperation for Progess in Latin America, published in June, 1961.

12

A Clinical Test: Latin America

To test out a new American foreign policy, freed of its fatal link to private investor interests, there could be no more appropriate area in the world of upheaval and present or future Folk War than the twenty countries of Latin America. Until 1958, they were considered perennially safe allies, either because of the iron grip of U.S.-allied dictators or because, in the half dozen more advanced countries, close economic ties kept their governments on friendly terms. They were considered private preserves until, with the outburst that greeted the visit of an American Vice-President, *anti-yanqui* sentiment bubbled up to the surface, bringing home to the United States the fact that the same tides of upheaval that were moving around the world, in the wide belt of "have-not" lands, were lapping also at the huge continent to the south.

Since then the tides have swelled; change was no longer on the surface only, through *coups d'etat* engineered by one or another investor-allied minority clique; change went deep, to the submerged majorities of the population. The minority groups' *coups d'etat* continued, here and there, on the surface, but underneath, the great majorities were awakening, stirred for the first time since the pioneering Mexican revolution of 1910. The cause of the awakening, as elsewhere in the underdeveloped world, was the fact that out of economic organization, created by the United States and the industrial West in alliance with the local ruling minorities, had come social organization and communication among the people. Reading and writing, radio, television, rapid travel over new roads and by air, the mushrooming factories, the vast plantations of coffee, sugar, bananas, cocoa, the impetus of World War II—all these factors, penetrating, organizing, developed a new social consciousness among the great out-groups, even to a degree among those in Peru, Ecuador, Bolivia, Paraguay, Guatemala, of isolated Indian culture, whose ancestors for thousands of years had suffered minority oppression in wooden silence.

The new developments went unnoticed by United States policy-makers, absorbed by the upheavals in exotic and faraway places. Latin America, as the Latin Americans of the minority cliques lamented to their

American partners, was taken for granted. When a split-off in the minority clique in Guatemala developed and the group taking over attempted to broaden its base among the Indian majority, encouraging them to press for wages as high as a dollar a day for their seasonal work in the banana plantations, the United States roused sufficiently to send in CIA agents, after the usual investor-planted propaganda about "communism," to organize the ousted wing of the minority clique to take power back again, in a routine *coup d'etat*. Nothing was indicated which the usual *coups d'etat*, engineered from time to time to keep the minority cliques properly in line, could not take care of.

Then suddenly, as 1959 came, several hundred Cubans destroyed the façade. The Cuban story will probably never be told in full; but it began when a Cuban intellectual, the typical rebellious student, fled to Mexico after attempting the usual futile revolt against dictatorship. In Mexico the Cuban student met a Spanish Republican, Alberto Bayo, a man with vast, although mostly academic, knowledge of guerrilla warfare. Bayo had read the works of Mao Tse-tung, not from ideological sympathy with the Chinese Communist, but because of his interest in the art of guerrilla warfare. From Mao, he had abstracted a basic idea: that guerrilla warfare in a peasant land must find its base among the peasants and move with them. The student, Fidel Castro, took what Bayo taught him and with the help of his "theoretician," Ernesto Guevara, applied it in Cuba. The result was the first folk war in the Americas (although Mexico's 1910 revolution had several of its qualities). The Cuban take-over by the Castro forces was not the usual *coup d'etat;* it shared with the Mexican revolt the characteristics of a majority rising, a genuine shift in the basis of power.

The nature of the Castro revolution made it plain that it could be overthrown only by genuine counter-revolution or full-scale invasion by a superior foreign power. The CIA, called upon once again, after the usual propaganda about communism by the displaced American investors, had in its files, available for study, a detailed analysis of the folk-war character of the Cuban revolution. Because of its peculiar ideological leanings, however, the CIA refused to accept this analysis; it proceeded to intervene on the same basis it had in Guatemala. The result was inevitable.

Out of the Cuban fiasco, however, came a degree of awakening among American policy-makers. Half a billion dollars were speedily routed through congressional approval for "social and economic development" in Latin America, plus another $100 million for "earthquake relief" in Chile. Senator Fulbright declared that it would be used "primarily to help the common man." Senator Gore rushed through amendments which, in theory, would keep the money from going directly to dictators, large landholders or rich tax-dodgers. Brazil, the key country, the coming power with seventy million people, was offered a special deal. Its new president, Jânio Quadros, awoke premonitions among American policy-makers when he said that his government would "never approve an aggression of any kind against Cuban sovereignty. Brazil will not accept that, in the name of continental solidarity, aggressive or punitive actions be taken against that nation. The principle to be observed in this case, within the system of continental cooperation, is above all the self-determination of peoples." After that, an international loan of nearly $2,000 million was arranged to underwrite Brazil's financial and economic recovery plan, $350 million of it directly from the United States.

The United States had good reason to look to Brazil. The huge, Portuguese-speaking country combined within its frontiers the elements of a new, democratic nationalism, based in the highly developed South, which might move toward a neutralist position and had already moved toward expanding trade with the communist world, long out of bounds; and also, in the underdeveloped, upheaval lands of its Northeast, the ingredients of a new folk war. If Brazil's Northeast were politically separate, instead of being a colony jointly exploited by the advanced South and United States investors, allied with the local minority cliques, it would undoubtedly be the next Latin American candidate for folk war. There, twenty million peasants live in conditions little different from serfdom on the vast estates of local *fazendeiros*. Under the leadership of a wild-haired lawyer, Francisco Julião, they banded together in huge peasant leagues along the lines first suggested, once again, by China's Mao, whom Julião, although by no means a Communist, visited. Julião also had long talks on peasant problems with Fidel Castro, whom he ardently supported. In contrast, he was never invited to the U.S. nor did any American with ideas on agrarian reform ever visit him. The over-all danger for American policy-makers in Brazil, however, was not the usual anticolonial revolt. It was the danger that the whole country, losing patience with American ignorance of things Brazilian (the august *New York Times*, in a two-column headline, placed the Brazilian former capital,

Rio de Janeiro, in Argentina) and uneasy under a growing, American-owned mortgage, might move toward a fully independent policy. This, in fact, appeared to be the aim of President Quadros during 1961.

A companion in the Brazilian trend was Mexico, restless again after two decades of "junior partnership" with the United States. Mexico's embryonic folk war, its 1910 revolution, was never quite completed, although it survived a series of United States counterattacks not unlike those made later on Cuba—the Pershing invasion of the north, the bombardment and capture of Veracruz and a propaganda campaign which, strangely, considering the difference in eras, was identical with that carried on against Cuba. It was largely Mexican remembrance of its own revolution and the American counterattack which led it to oppose, along with Brazil and Ecuador, U. S. plans for condemnation of Castro. Mexico, partly because it already had a great upheaval, partly because it still retained a degree of control over American investors, was also, at least temporarily, safe from the folk war. In a population of some thirty-two million, there was significant unrest only among sections of the non-Hispanicized Indian population, reduced by urban assimilation to fewer than seven million by 1960. The minority clique in Mexico, although closely allied with American investors and in control of the nation's press, did not have political control, which was still vested in the heirs of the Mexican revolution through an intricate, one-party system. The government thus served as a buffer between majority out-group and the "economic elite," who had not quite regained their traditional status as power elite. A folk war trend in Mexico would thus have no concrete objective under conditions resem-

149

bling guardianship of majority interests. Despite all-out obedience to American policy in the press, the peculiar nature of the Mexican set-up tended to move it, like Brazil, toward an independent policy.

In the rest of Latin America, except for temporary exceptions which sprang up from time to time, even though economic conditions varied greatly, the normal pattern of social relationships typical of underdeveloped areas and upheaval lands prevailed. A split in the power elite, however, characterized two of the most advanced countries, Argentina and Uruguay, and also Venezuela, Colombia and Ecuador; one group moved toward democratization, another toward retention of power, or, as in Uruguay, toward reinforcement of privilege previously weakened. In regimes under the direct control of American investors—Nicaragua, Guatemala, Honduras, Paraguay—outright or covert dictatorships used force to keep down occasional protest; in countries where investor control was exerted more discreetly but nonetheless firmly—Peru, Chile—unrest among the impoverished masses was channeled off. In Chile, it was done through alternate elections of the "right" or "left" wing of the power elite; in Peru through cultivation of a dying "mass movement" (the Apristas) as an escape valve. In countries such as Bolivia unpredictable trends developed, since little mass awakening had as yet taken place; or, as in Costa Rica, a contrary trend occurred, with the gradual relinquishing of a previous mass basis by the power elite. Except for Argentina, Uruguay and to a degree Costa Rica, with more advanced populations, these countries were characterized by all pre-folk-war conditions: A close alliance between local power elite and foreign investors, versus a vast outgroup majority, poverty-stricken, diseased and still largely illiterate, needing only a little more organization and a spark. In this group also was El Salvador, in the throes of internecine disputes among its power elite; on the fringes were Haiti, a law unto itself, too sunk in poverty even for organized protest; the Dominican Republic, where preconditions of folk war, developing after the assasination of its dictator, were held in check; and Panama, restless but impotent beside the Canal.

For this mass of tinder, Cuba did indeed provide a spark, but no great wind arose to fan the flames, although small fires began to smolder. The Soviet Union, moving with extraordinary caution in this private preserve of the United States, concentrated its efforts on Cuba, countering hypothetical U. S. threats of attack with answering threats of hypothetical rockets, U. S. economic blockade with economic aid, propaganda with propaganda, U. S. arms for refugees with Czech arms for Castro, limiting itself cautiously to checking maneuvers. The Soviet Union's ultimate objective, probably, was to use Cuba as a spearhead for an all-out propaganda drive in Latin America to fan the smoldering fires of mass unrest. But for the moment, the Soviet Union's objectives were, from its standpoint, strictly defensive, in terms of global strategy; its plan was to build up Cuba militarily so that attacks on Castro would be costly, then let the Cuban regime find its own immediate course, perhaps moving toward neutralism, as Castro had planned.

It is probable that the Soviet Union, for the time being, would prefer a neutralist Latin America to one in the Soviet orbit; the Russians do not have sufficient economic capacity to counter American moves throughout the hemisphere, and they dare not bring their military potential to bear. A neutralist Latin America would serve for the present and would be an effective barrier to any United States action along the lines it took in Cuba, via the CIA, since neutral Latin American governments, allied with the Afro-Asian bloc, would bring down United Nations condemnation of the United States and possible sanctions. The Soviet Union would like nothing better, short of total elimination of the U. S.; and we may presume that this is its aim for the present. This happens also to be the aim of the Afro-Asian bloc in the United Nations, busy courting Latin American delegates, and the tentative direction of Mexico and Brazil—the leaders of Latin America—as well as, temporarily, of Ecuador. United States policy-makers, of course, have not thought of this possibility.

Within the framework of a limited analysis, in which the basic factor, the alliance between U. S. investors and Latin America's minority ruling groups, was carefully ignored, the latest United States policy toward Latin America, as enunciated by President Kennedy and sundry administration spokesmen in 1961, was considered a step forward. Under a rather double-edged slogan, "*Progreso, sí, tiranía, no,*" a fairly broad ten-year program was proclaimed with an objective described as "to satisfy the basic needs of the people of the Americas for homes, work, land, health and schools," and not described as to meet the hemispheric challenge laid down in Cuba by the Castro-inaugurated economic reforms there.

The "Kennedy Plan" is essentially the "Galbraith Plan." John Kenneth Galbraith, a fashionable American economist, outlined it as part of an approach to the economic problems of underdeveloped areas, prepared for Kennedy as a presidential candidate in late 1960; Galbraith's reward was the ambassadorship to India, where presumably he could test his theories on the ground. Galbraith's thesis was that pouring dollars into underdeveloped areas would not do any economic good so long as the dollars merely fattened those who were already fat, as had been the case; he had figured out that the dollars could do good only in countries with an educated people, a skilled managerial group running the administration and the projects, and an honest, effective government with a sense of social justice and with constructive aims. Dollars sent in otherwise, he asserted, would simply enrich the rich and stiffen the status quo.

The thesis was not incorrect; although, practically speaking, it would have eliminated all underdeveloped areas as recipients of dollars if it were put into effect literally—countries with an educated people, a skilled managerial group and a good government are not underdeveloped. The central idea, however, that United States aid be administered so as to foster the basic conditions for economic growth, in areas such as Latin America, was germane and not unlike the notion that God helps those who help themselves. This, of course, had been the announced purpose of all U. S. economic aid since outright relief grants had ended after World War II; it was Galbraith's suggestion that the purpose actually be carried through that was new.

As announced by President Kennedy, however, the Galbraith Plan for Latin America sounded daring. Kennedy offered sizable and long-term dollar assistance provided the Latin American recipients would make "determined efforts" to help themselves. "They and they alone," Kennedy said of the Latin American countries, "can mobilize their resources, enlist the energies of their people and modify their social patterns, so that all, and not just a privileged few, share in the fruits of growth."

Under conditions of that kind, Kennedy said, the United States would advance sums to help each country devise development and reform plans, support economic integration projects, study commodity market problems, establish scientific, medical and agricultural projects, increase technical training and cultural exchange and in general work for social progress, including land reform, general education and housing. In ten years of this effort, Kennedy indicated, as much as $13,000 million could flow to Latin America, half of it in *private* capital.

This sum was slightly more than the total amount of American private capital invested in Latin America and registered; the entry of nearly half again as much private U. S. capital, unless carefully balanced by competing capital from other countries and under solid Latin American controls, would create an American economic hegemony in Latin America that would make our late control in Cuba pallid by comparison. The suggestion that half of American assistance be in the form of further economic occupation by American investors was not greeted kindly by nationalist statesmen in Brazil, Mexico, Argentina, Venezuela, Ecuador and Colombia, and was received with ambivalence elsewhere. Latin Americans are just as aware as North Americans that private capital does not go into business for reasons other than profit-making; and the drain on Latin America's dollars through departing profits, many of them in the direction of Switzerland, had for some years been

154

a principal complaint. (A Department of Commerce Latin American Investment Survey some years ago indicated, discreetly, that more dollars were leaving Latin America as profit than were entering as investment; and that was during a period of high investment there by American financiers.) The lopsided condition of the over-all balance of payments for countries such as Brazil, as opposed to a fair balance of trade with the United States, the continuing pile-up of payments for services, interest, imports, freight and profits, plus occasional payments on the principal of debts, has made many Latin Americans doubtful about new foreign investments in high-profit fields—where, of course, they automatically go unless strict controls are put in force.

The other half of the monetary aspect of the Kennedy proposal was received by most Latin Americans with some enthusiasm, slightly tempered by charges, among the "anti-yanquis," that it was a bribe. Latin America's basic problems dealing with present conditions, not future planning, are three: Disease, illiteracy, and big landholders. It has innumerable other problems, including transport, inflation, poor housing, low wages, high prices, superstition, dictators, and an inordinate number of crooks in high places, proportionately more perhaps than the United States. The Kennedy proposal at least gave honorary mention to some of the main problems, a rare feat in such cases. Previous American proposals for "helping" Latin America had been limited almost exclusively to offers of loans to pay debts owed to American exporters or investors; or for construction of projects owned by Americans; or, to bolster the ruling cliques, sums for military spending on semisurplus American equipment which totaled about $400 million. Some of our surplus crops were also sold to Latin American countries in short supply, at bargain prices in their local currencies, much to the rage of competing exporters such as Uruguay and Argentina. The Kennedy proposal, especially as amplified at the Punta del Este meeting, was seen as a correct step by Latin Americans still hoping for a return to the Good Neighbor Policy adopted by the U.S. in World War II when we desperately needed Latin American raw materials.

In synthesis, the conditions of upheaval were present in many Latin American countries; there was a growing trend for the leading nations among them to move toward a policy independent of the United States, a trend which the Soviet Union hoped to foster, partly through Cuban example; the United States moved to counteract the upheaval threat and the "independentist" trend by offers of large-scale assistance, including, for the first time, some basic assistance; and Latin Americans, with some dubiousness, waited to see what would happen.

Will the United States policy succeed in its objective, the countering of the upheaval threat and the independentist trend? The answer has to be a somewhat qualified "no," qualified only in the sense that the United States move, although late, may delay the drift of Latin America long enough for an effective policy to be worked out and applied.

The reason the present American policy, the Kennedy-Galbraith Plan, will not fundamentally modify the Latin American trend is that it fails to take into account that the alliance between American investors and local Latin American minority cliques, including dictators, will effectively block any attempt at "democratization" in any area controlled by the alliance; moreover, the proposed flood into Latin America of more private American capital will increase the strength of that alliance under present circumstances, with a reactive growth in the strength of upheaval forces. Surface modification of the trend may result, temporarily, in some areas, because contribution toward health, education, land reform—all visible factors—will offer hope. But for these contributions to make a lasting penetration, they will have to be magnified even beyond the imagination of either Mr. Kennedy or Mr. Galbraith, as thus far demonstrated. In Brazil alone, seventeen million adults suffer from leishmaniasis, a virulent and disfiguring infection that, apart from human loss, causes an immeasurable loss in economic productivity; treatment for this disease is available; an American-made drug called fungizone will do the job. The cost, per curative treatment, is about $100. The cost of curing seventeen million people of this one infection is therefore $1,700 million. What part of the $500 million of government funds voted for all Latin America up to September 1961, to take care of all projects, including health, will the $1,700 million come out of? As far as the basic problems of Latin America are concerned, the Kennedy-Galbraith plan is not even a palliative.

Democratization by these methods may be presumed to be impossible, however excellent the intention. The basic rule holds: In an area where there is not enough to go around, the privileged group cannot be expected to yield any privilege. Democratization cannot be imposed from the top down; the only way Latin America will democratize is through its own people, through the elimination of the present alliance between American "ownership" capital and the local power elite and the absorption or removal of ruling minorities of all kinds. If the United States will help in this, through the methods previously described, it will then be able to count on the people of Latin America as allies in any struggle with the Soviet Union and its fake solutions. If the United States will not help, then the people of Latin America will accept any allies they can get, as the United States did in its Revolution, when it allied itself with the most reactionary regime on earth, the corrupt monarchy of France, or as Cuba did more recently, following the same pattern.

PART 4

NUCLEAR SHIELD, JEFFERSONIAN SWORD

We have failed to recognize sufficiently that it takes more than
dollars to win the cold war.

— Sen. Karl E. Mundt

As quoted in Reader's
Digest, February, 1961.

13

The Overriding Problem

So far we have seen how the Soviet Union, by
manipulation of the new "people power" in the upheaval
lands, has been able, within the delicate conditions of
military stand-off, to upset the balance of forces and
win a dangerous advantage over the United States.

We have observed how a series of small losses on
the "people front," totaling a grave and continuing defeat, have been a product of our immobility in foreign
policy and the flaws in our instruments of policy formation and enforcement, our intelligence services, our
propaganda agency and the fledgling "little war" that
would answer the "folk war."

We have indicated how our immobility in foreign

161

policy, as contrasted with the mobility of the Soviet Union, has come about because, in effect, our foreign policy has been dictated, not by our national interests, but by the private interests of one pressure group only, our overseas investors. We have explained how, for economic reasons, our investors are bound to the declining minority cliques in the upheaval lands and, in turn, bind America to them, placing us fatally on the losing side.

We have recommended that our foreign policy be freed from the grip of private overseas ownership interests before the continuing small losses add up to total defeat and that it be reformed, remade in the interest of the nation as a whole; and we have suggested tentative ways in which this might be done.

Our premise has been that if these steps were taken, if patriotism and also sacrifice enough could be aroused, the United States could then, by taking the side of the people in the upheaval lands, undo the damage our foreign policy has done, reverse the advance of the Soviet Union and finally overbalance it on the same front on which it has overbalanced the United States so far. This objective, while basic to any success in our foreign policy, would nevertheless be only the beginning.

There would remain overriding problems, problems which will be with us until the conflict between the Soviet Union and the United States is finally resolved—either suddenly, through mutual destruction or unilateral explosion, or eventually, through erosion of one side or the other, or both, by time; or through the arrival of new governing factors for the race of mankind, new elements beyond predictability or extrapolation.

Reduced to their simplest, the overriding problems

are three questions. The first is: What shall we do about the stalemate? Does the nuclear stand-off, necessarily expanded to a balance in all areas of conventional warfare, favor the Soviet Union or the United States? Should we consider the stalemate a barrier to our efforts to overcome the threat of the Soviet Union or, just possibly, a device which, properly made use of, could enable us to win?

The second question and the third are part of each other: What are we fighting against? And what are we fighting for? Is it enough to say that we are fighting "against communism," or "for capitalism"? What is the nature of the enemy? What is our own nature? Many books have been published, millions upon millions of words written about the Soviet Union and now about China. Have any of them really told us what we are fighting against? Of all the statesmen and politicians and editors and authors and clergymen who have urged us to die for Americanism, have any of them defined it? Do we really know what we are about?

We believe the time has come for these overriding problems to be considered; and we shall consider them in the following final two chapters in what might be called a seminal way: We hope to plant seeds which will burgeon in American minds to produce study and eventually lead to understanding, particularly of what we should and must fight for, and not only abroad. We need to know who and what we are even more than we need to know the enemy.

Let us consider first the problem of the stalemate, which—complicated though it is and meriting not a chapter but many volumes—is perhaps easier to dissect and answer, if looked at freshly, than the other problems of self-analysis.

163

Our security may be lost piece by piece, country by country, without the firing of a single missile or the crossing of a single border.

— *President John F. Kennedy*

Talk at Eighth National Conference on International Economic and Social Progress, Washington, June 16, 1961.

14

Advantage of Stalemate

The military stand-off between the United States and the Soviet Union, on the level of nuclear and conventional war, has so far been viewed by most American strategists as an obstacle to enforcement of foreign policy, or, in some extreme and anachronistic cases, has been wished out of existence. However, if we look at the problem newly, accepting the stalemate as a part of reality, though delicately and shakily balanced, we come upon a perhaps surprising possibility: There is nothing to prevent the United States from using the stalemate as a nuclear shield, sheltered by which we can easily maneuver on other fronts, once our psychological block is removed and our foreign policy revised so as to enable us to use a Jeffersonian weapon—the people, particularly the people of the upheaval lands. These are the people the Soviet Union is now maneuvering and manipulating, in "concentration-point" tactics, to produce repeated defeats for American policy-makers.

Working around the edges of our nuclear shield, we could turn the military stand-off into an unprecedented advantage in applying a renovated foreign policy; then, far from being an obstacle, it would give us a freedom in policy enforcement enjoyed by no other nation in history except Rome after defeat of Carthage and, for geographical reasons, ancient China. If neither side dare destroy the other for fear of self-destruction, then, in fact, we have peace, however delicately balanced, so far as all-out military clash is concerned; so long as that balance is maintained, we should be limited only by our degree of strategic astuteness on every other front of conflict with the Soviet Union. What would happen to the Soviet Union and their allies if, instead of gaining the many small victories they register now in the hope of adding them up to a totality of victory, they were suddenly to begin to lose, to sustain defeat after defeat? It should be recalled that a tenet of Marxism, intrinsic in Soviet and Chinese strategy, is never to attack a superior power head-on, but to nibble away at it. The stalemate, turned into nuclear shield, would enable us to bring our corrected foreign-policy instrumentalities into play at every point—without danger of global war— and with discreet propaganda maneuvering, to drive the enemy to its own doors. We could meet each thrust

165

with a better one of our own and seize the initiative. This is an objective to be sought; we contend that it can be attained.

Moreover, it is plainly in the national interest of the United States to maintain zealously the military stand-off with the Soviet Union—so long as we cannot achieve the increasingly wide margin of superiority needed to make possible a victory in this deadly field. As was noted in the first chapter, in nuclear warfare with heavy weapons there can be *arithmetical* superiority, that is, one side may accumulate more hydrogen-bomb warheads than the other, and so on; but there cannot be, at this technological stage, any possibility of *factual* superiority. All-out nuclear warfare under present conditions of mutual suicide would be a psychopathic, not a military, objective. All of our top strategists, even those who talk differently in public, are well aware of this fact. Of course, some diplomats, who fortunately do not make policy, still ignore reality, moving along in a peculiar dream world in which the danger of nuclear destruction applies only to the Soviet Union. Here are some remarks by such a "senior American diplomat," actually reported in 1961:

"Mr. Khrushchev should be asked if he really wants to risk Moscow for Vientiane or Leningrad for Saigon or Peiping (Peking) for Bangkok. Mr. Khrushchev should be told that so long as America can destroy Moscow, Peiping, Hanoi, in the twinkling of an eye, it does not fear the Soviet Union no matter how many missiles or spacemen it has. Because the main point is that the Soviet Union cannot use its power against the United States for one overwhelming reason: the knowledge that America's counterattack would destroy Russia."

This is a blindness, a unilateral blockage, which we may be certain Mr. Khrushchev does not share. The fact is that a nuclear attack unleashed by either side, under existing circumstances, would spell destruction for both. Is the senior diplomat saying that only the Soviet Union would be destroyed? This is the type of dream-world thinking and nuclear bomb-rattling which, however many Russian or American "senior diplomats" engage in it, no longer even has propaganda value, except, perhaps, among Civil Defense dependents or manufacturers of fall-out shelter "crackers," or conceivably, our new-model pacifists who climb aboard nuclear submarines for beatnik kicks.

For all strategic purposes it must be recognized, above all by American policy-shapers, that a nuclear stalemate exists which will continue until a breakthrough is made into new defensive or offensive technology or until an accident happens. Beyond all doubt, as a matter of national survival, it is in the direct interest of the United States to prevent any break in the stalemate, either in perpetuity or until such time as the United States, by a means not now available, can defend itself from destruction.

This life-or-death fact has been recognized even by military men who once pushed for a showdown with the Soviet Union, such as General Douglas MacArthur, who in two of his "final addresses," one in New York, the other in East Lansing, Michigan, declared that the awesome potential of modern weapons had "destroyed the possibility of global war as a medium for international settlement of differences." The weapons, he observed, made it "impossible even for the winner" to turn war into anything but destruction for winner and loser alike.

167

"No longer," he said, "can global warfare be a successful weapon of international adventure. If you win, you stand only to lose." Such warfare, he said, "contains now only the germs of double suicide." This is why Robert MacNamara, Defense Secretary, put into motion in 1961 means of preventing what he called "false-alarm war" by reducing United States dependence on "hair-trigger retaliation." He noted that "in the present state of the art" of electronic and other types of warning systems, the United States could not be "wholly sure of unambiguous warning." These efforts were directed at false alarm that might lead us to "retaliate" *before* Soviet attack; could the point of potential mutual nuclear destruction be made any clearer? Plainly, at the top level, American strategists were exerting every effort to preserve the stalemate with the Soviet Union to any point short of technological breakthrough, a point not envisaged in factual terms, despite the new "neutron bomb" potential.

It would seem clear, therefore, that we may presume that immediate military danger to the United States arises, not from stalemate, *but from the possibility of its interruption*—a danger which the United States and the Soviet Union share.

We come now to a paradox: The only logical deduction is that both we and the Russians have a common interest in keeping up each other's ability for nuclear attack and defense, for maintaining the respective capacities approximately equal.

Considering the global harvest the winner would have in the contest between the Soviet Union and the United States—if there could be a winner—would not a decline in Soviet retaliatory capacity, for example, provide an extraordinary temptation for the United States to attack and destroy the Russian military potential, thus cutting the Gordian knot? Would not a decline in the retaliatory capacity of the United States offer a similar, even more certain temptation for the Soviet Union? So long as a factual parity is maintained, however, attack would be a fearsome risk, for even the remnants of retaliatory capacity on either side would be enough to ensure that the half-dead victor would thereafter be a second-rate power, subject, moreover, to criminal proceedings instituted by the civilized world that remained.

Peace can be kept and national survival guaranteed, therefore, only by the paradoxical maintenance of Soviet nuclear-weapon capacity, for defense especially, on approximately the same level as our own. Of course, it would be too paradoxical to suggest that the United States and the Soviet Union share their latest nuclear defenses; it would, however, startling as it sounds, be not illogical as a means of preserving the stalemate; and the stalemate is, beyond doubt, vital at this time to the national existence of both powers.

To the degree that the United States can rely on a continuing military stalemate with the Soviet Union, then, always within conditions of minute-by-minute preparedness, it can have, if it will, a free hand to explore the advantages of nonmilitary means of foreign-policy enforcement, to use the key nonmilitary bases for global strategy. On this level—always assuming a corrected foreign policy—the United States could have a wide advantage. The Soviet Union does not have the same degree or quality of opportunity, although it recognized the chance of advantage to be gained in these circumstances well in advance of the United States. The reason is that the Soviet Union, regardless of its inflated propaganda claims, is far inferior to the United States economically, on a global scale; it does not have the resources to back up opposed policies. That is why it uses the "concentration point" method of attack; it is, as explained, the tactic of an inferior force, not a superior one.

If the United States, after due but, hopefully, speedy consideration, finally corrects its foreign policy to enable us to use the "Jeffersonian Sword" of people-power, that is, if it separates national interest from investor-group pressures, would it then have the machinery to put its policy into operation? Assuming that the all-important problem of personnel in our intelligence services is corrected at the same time, we can be increasingly hopeful of American enforcement machinery. Functional improvement—although still, of course, within the limits of erroneous policy—was observable in 1961. A refurbished "operations" center was established to keep liaison twenty-four hours a day among all key agencies having to do with foreign-policy developments or procedures, thus for the first time since shortly after World War II enabling rapid action instead of red-tape snarl when emergencies might arise. An expanded network of interdepartmental task forces was set up to handle individual trouble spots. Controls over subaltern action—undoubtedly one of the weakest points in execution of effective policy all through the Eisenhower administration—were greatly increased.

Particularly important, in view of the mistake-multiplication that was evident in such cases as Cuba or Laos, was the attempt to prevent the accumulation of small errors on lower levels which marked foreign-policy formation in the past. However, policy is still made much as it has been, through informal talks among agency heads and between each of them and the President or one of his close advisers; the principal difference has been that the consequences of courses of action are more thoroughly examined. This informal arrangement has lately been complicated by the very expansion of "task forces" in the field, which has blocked many "traditional" channels and tended to throw more and more of the burden even for detail decisions on the President or the Secretary of State. Because of this factor, the limited area of decision-making for details, American foreign-policy influences have become personalized. Ideas in 1961, for example, flowed through a small group —Soviet specialist Charles Bohlen, Senate Foreign Relations Committee Chairman Fulbright, special White House assistants McGeorge Bundy and Walt Rostow, Latin American expert Berle, Robert Kennedy, former Secretary of State Dean Acheson, Secretary Rusk, of course, and scattered "non-specialists," such as the "presidential brains" Ted Sorenson and Richard Goodwin. It will be noted that none of these "pipelines," including Latin American expert Berle, ever publicly expressed any understanding of the need for a mobile American foreign policy that could move with the rising tide of majority upheaval, although an inkling of the need may have come to Senator Fulbright after the Cuban fiasco in April 1961.

However, if we assume an eventual recognition of the prerequisities for American victory on the nonmilitary front, during a period of military stalemate between

171

the United States and the Soviet Union, the foreign-policy-making mechanism could be effective. A renovated intelligence agency would provide the facts; an evaluation board of area specialists would go over the facts and interpret them; an allied strategy board would decide courses of action, considering the objectives and consequences of each; and the decision to act, not act, or call for further checking and evaluation could then be made on a solid basis by the Secretary of State and the President and their advisers, in consultation. The enforcement mechanisms, which would consist mainly of propaganda and economic weapons, with exceptional and carefully limited use of the "little war" technique only where we were sure of the ground, could then be set in motion in line with the specific requirements of any given world area.

The first step, nevertheless, in taking advantage of the new circumstances of military stalemate, would be to clean house, get rid of the accumulation of cog-thinkers and representatives of foreign-investor interests who have provoked the present mess in foreign policy. This is what an aroused American public opinion should demand.

If adjustment is not made to take advantage of the opportunities the stalemate provides, then the Soviet Union, already in the lead, can continue to make use of its inferior forces to overwhelm the United States, with its control over the "people power" at each concentration point the Soviet Union selects. The result, as has been noted, would be the gradual elimination of the United States as a world force and our eventual isolation or quarantine within a "Fortress America," subject to internal collapse by resulting pressures. If adjustment

172

is made, then the military stalemate can in effect shelter the United States, with due caution. Meanwhile bold maneuvers can be undertaken in the upheaval areas of the world to reverse the drift of the majority movements toward Soviet alliance by default. Instead we can make use of our superior economic capacities to guide these movements into new, voluntary alliances with us, in their national interest. At the very least, a policy that would move America with the tide instead of against it would enable us to block the Soviet Union around the edges of the nuclear barrier between us, and would certainly prevent any new penetration of the area that most vitally concerns us—Latin America. In fact, a foreign policy based on people, carried out in conditions of enforced "non-war," need not be restricted to the upheaval areas; as noted, it could be applied, step by step, on the non-military level, to the Soviet Union and China, once we find ourselves on the right side and moving with the tide.

These are circumstances in which the military stalemate should be nurtured; for practical purposes—if our other policy-enforcing measures are effective, of course —it serves us every bit as much, and probably more, than would outright victory over the Soviet Union, even if that were possible without our own destruction. Without the stalemate, even a correct policy based on "people power" and achieving major victories on that front would eventually come up against the threat of military reprisal by the Soviet Union.

The future of the stalemate is, of course, beyond prediction at this time; it could continue, if we work at it, well into the interplanetary age. The neutron bomb, although adding temptations, need not interrupt it; a neutron bomb is essentially a large-scale tactical

173

weapon; the overriding fact of total nuclear destructive capacities remains as a deterrent to anything short of instantaneous elimination of retaliatory power. We may yet turn to the paradox we mentioned—the sharing of defensive weapons between the United States and the Soviet Union—as a mutual guarantee against national suicide; there is little doubt that such an unprecedented "partnership" with the enemy would be in our national interest if we had mobility of maneuver on the non-stalemated fronts of foreign-policy operation.

To continue the speculation, it may be considered reasonably certain that any "breakthrough" in the stalemate will not come from "offensive" weapons, however superscientific; retaliation with present weapons would still prohibit victory. We may imagine, therefore, that a rupture will come only from the development of new "defensive" devices (or from accident or madness). Which again leads us back to our paradox, the strange need to share, perhaps through the United Nations if that body could be made to function, our equipment for defense; and to work toward agreement with the Soviet Union, not toward disarmament, an even more impossible aim, but toward international policing, on a tripartite "troika" or any other basis that would *guarantee* surety of information, of mutual defense parity.

Until a nuclear-defense breakthrough occurs, it is logical to assume that the stalemate can be our shield and our opportunity. If we can combine our "nuclear shield" with our "Jeffersonian Sword," hopefully described in the next and final chapter, we shall not only have what might be called a "Damoclean Peace," as now, but a chance to build a peace that could, in a new era of democracy, of "people rule," endure long enough for mankind to mature and rise at last from savagery.

174

I submit that there can be no other national goals than the ones in the Declaration of Independence.

— *Sen. Barry Goldwater*

Commencement address, Long
Island University, June 9, 1961.

15

What Is America For and Against?

In times of stress, such as those through which America is now passing, there is a tendency to escape from harsh realities into softer fantasy; to disguise fear under an outer cover of another emotion, such as hatred or even an apparent patriotism; to lay our troubles at the door of others; and to seek refuge from thought in the use of word symbols that represent emotions rather than meanings. Mere wishing, however, will not make anything come to pass; and we cannot win the people of the world to our side in the struggle with the Soviet Union through fantasies, emotions and empty word symbols. If we can remake our foreign policy and take advantage of the nuclear stalemate to shape it into a barrier against the Soviet Union instead of the United States, finally gaining access to the people of the world, what shall we say to them? What is America for and against?

So far, in our discussion of the remaking of American foreign policy, we have tried to brush out of our way the accumulations of cant and fancy and get down to the heart of what is wrong. Now, in discussing what America is for and against, we shall try to expose layers so deep, indeed, that at times they may seem to be the substance itself; to penetrate, not to what is wrong, but to what is right, to the America our forefathers founded and nurtured in blood and pain and love. First, let us scrub off the layers.

In Russia and China the populace is whipped into frenzy, when occasion demands, over the "cannibalism of capitalism" by techniques not far different from those used in the United States to arouse the nation against the "cancer of communism." In the Soviet Union "freedom" and "democracy" are equated with "'communism"; in the United States the same words, "freedom" and "democracy," are equated with "capitalism." What are "capitalism," "communism," "freedom," "democracy"?

A dictionary defines capitalism as "an economic system in which the means of production are privately owned and goods are produced for profit, usually under competitive conditions"; it defines communism as "a classless system of society in which the community owns the means of production and aims at an equitable distribution of wealth"; freedom is defined as "exemption from power or control by another"; democracy is described as "a form of government vesting sovereignty in the people, who exercise it either directly or through elected representatives."

Consider these definitions rather than the emotions we attach to the respective word symbols. It is immediately plain that for the Russians, Chinese or any other people on earth no such thing as "communism" exists. It is equally plain that for the great majority of Americans who do not own means of production, a Capitalist is some other fellow. And freedom? How many Americans or Russians have freedom in this exact sense of being "exempt from power or control by another"? Or democracy? Americans and Russians both "elect" representatives, but who "selects" them? How many Americans chose Kennedy to run for the presidency? How many Russians selected Khrushchev to run for his chairmanship? Is the difference in kind or in degree?

For that matter, are we any more "capitalist," in the exact definition of the word, than the Russians are "communist"? European economists have recently expressed amazement, not over the differences, but over the similarities of the Soviet and the American economies. In the Soviet Union, production and distribution are controlled by huge trusts which employ a majority of the urban population; and in the United States, production and distribution are controlled by huge corporations which employ a majority of the urban population. From packaging-room employee through typist and memo-pusher up to and including the managerial level, the only difference reported between American and Russian, in their work, is the language and a greater American efficiency.

The typical American corporation is run by managers selected by directors selected mainly by banks which hold majority voting rights or by other corporations; the typical Russian trust is run by managers selected by directors selected mainly by a central ministry or bureau whose faceless personnel are named by other faceless personnel. Trusts and corporations are both headless monsters owned by no one; in other words, neither is *privately* owned. The day of the individual self-made tycoon, the Astors, the Goulds, the Morgans, the original Rockefeller, is as dead in America as it is in the Soviet Union. Individual capitalism as it now exists in America is represented by the corner grocery store, soon to give way to the chain; or by the small farmer, soon to yield to the "factory in the field." It is as close to extinction as those remnants of individual capitalism that linger in the Soviet Union, legally persecuted in the shadow of the great trusts, as profiteering or speculation.

To seek out a basic difference between the Soviet Union and the United States, and to penetrate to what America really is for and against, we shall obviously have to seek out firmer ground than a theoretical "capitalism" or "communism." The difference is more fundamental even than economics; it is in essence the oldest dispute in the history of mankind. Let us state now what America is for and against:

America, as it was founded, was for the rights of the individual man, the basis of people power; and it was against abrogation of those rights by the state. The Soviet Union, as it was founded, was for the rights of the new state, that is, the faceless totality of the nation, and against the rights of the individual man, "reserved" for a future epoch. To the degree that the United States still represents in its way of life the rights of the individual man, and bases itself on those rights in its approach to the peoples of the world, and to the degree that the Soviet Union continues to represent, in its way of life, the abrogation of those rights by the state, to that degree we are certain of victory if we will only use the people power and not let it go by default.

There is no need to "invent" an American creed for propaganda purposes; there is a need to revitalize and make known to the world the creed we were born with and from. Let us put it together from Thomas Jefferson's own words:

The doctrines of Europe were that men in numerous association could not be restrained within the limits of order and justice, but by forces, physical and moral, wielded over them by authorities independent of their will. To constrain the people, they deemed it necessary to keep them down by hard labor, poverty and ignorance, and to take from them, as from bees, so much of their earnings that unremitting labor would be necessary to obtain a sufficient surplus barely to sustain a scanty and miserable life. Our doctrine, on the contrary, was to maintain the will of the majority and of the people themselves. We believed with

179

them that man was a rational animal, endowed by nature with rights and with an innate sense of justice, and that he could be restrained from wrong and protected in right by moderate powers, confided to persons of his own choice and held to their duties by dependence on his own will. We believed that men habituated to think for themselves and to follow their reason as their guide would be more easily and safely governed than they would be with minds nourished in error, vitiated and debased by ignorance, indigence and oppression.

Sometimes it is said that man cannot be trusted with government of himself. Can he then be trusted with the government of others? Or have we found angels in the form of rulers to govern him? In every government on earth there is some trace of human weakness, some germ of corruption and degeneracy; every government degenerates when trusted to the rulers alone. The people, therefore, are its only safe depositories; and the influence over government must be shared by all the people. If every individual who composes their mass participates in the ultimate authority, the government will be safe. It has been thought that corruption is restrained by confining the right of suffrage to a few of the wealthier people—but it would be more effectually restrained by extension of that right to such numbers as would bid defiance to any means of corruption.

We think experience has proved it safer for the mass of individuals composing society to reserve to themselves, personally, the exercise of all rightful powers, delegating those in which they are not competent to deputies named—and removable—by themselves immediately. The weak and craven, the rich and corrupt, see more safety and accessibility in a strong executive; the healthy, firm and virtuous, feeling confidence in their own physical and moral resources, are willing to part with only so much power as is necessary for their good government and, therefore, to retain the rest in the hands of the many. Do not be frightened into the surrender of true principles by the alarms of the timid or the croakings of wealth against the ascendency of the people. All power is inherent in the people.

Educate and inform the whole mass of the people. Enable them to see that it is in their interest to preserve peace and order, and they will preserve them. They are the only sure reliance for the preservation of our liberty. Truth is great and will prevail if left to herself; she is the proper and sufficient antagonist to error and has nothing to fear from the conflict, unless by human interposition she is disarmed of her natural weapons, free argument and debate. If there be any among us who would wish to dissolve this union or to change its republican form, let them stand undisturbed as monuments to the safety with which error of opinion may be tolerated where reason is left free to combat it.

The first principle of republicanism

is that majority rule is the fundamental
law of every society of individuals with
equal rights; but all, too, will bear in
mind this sacred principle, that though
the will of the majority is in all cases to
prevail, that will, to be rightful, must be
reasonable; and that the minority possess
their equal rights which equal laws must
protect, and to violate them would be
oppression. No man has a natural right
to commit aggression on the equal rights
of another, and this is all from which
laws ought to restrain him; every man is
under the natural duty of contributing
to the necessities of society, and this is
all the laws should enforce on him.

The flames kindled on the 4th of July,
1776, have spread over too much of the
globe to be extinguished by the feeble
engines of despotism; on the contrary,
they will consume those engines and all
who work them. May the Declaration of
Independence be to the world, to some
sooner, to others later, but finally to all,
the signal of arousing men to burst the

chains under which monkish ignorance and superstition had persuaded them to bind themselves, and to assume the blessings and security of self-government, restoring the free right to unbounded exercise of reason and freedom of opinion. All eyes are opened or are opening to the rights of man. The general spread of the light of knowledge has already laid open, for all to see, the palpable truth: that the mass of mankind has not been born with saddles on their backs, nor a favored few booted and spurred, ready to ride them legitimately by the grace of God.

These words of Jefferson were the heart of the creed that America was born with and can survive with; we need it first of all for ourselves; then, as instruments to defend it, we can place our reliance on the mighty weapons of peace and war we should have at our command to meet the threat of the "engines of despotism." America's creed is not a theoretical "capitalism"; it is the people, the ultimate reality; faith in people is what has distinguished our Republic from every government in the world for nearly two centuries. How, then, have we allowed the Soviet Union to overbalance us, to place itself "on the side" of the people who are struggling to put into practice the Jeffersonian

184

principle of majority rule through equal rights for all, and to maneuver us, little war, intelligence, information, our whole instrumentality of policy, onto the side of the "booted and spurred"? Have we listened to "the croakings of wealth against the ascendancy of the people"? Have we forgotten that "all power is inherent in the people"? If we finally betray our own principles, then the "last, best hope for mankind" will be shattered; our struggle with the Soviet Union and its allies will be nothing more than another historical collision of two empires, greedily disputing the world as two hyenas fight over a piece of carrion; and sooner or later the aroused people of the world will take up the invincible weapon we discarded and eliminate both.

What is America for and against? We are for our own people and all the people in the world; we are against all who oppress them or would oppress them at home or abroad; and we believe with Thomas Jefferson that "we cannot deny to other nations that principle whereon our government is founded, that every nation has the right to govern itself internally under what forms it pleases and to change those forms at its own will."

On this Jeffersonian rock was laid the foundation of all that America has been or can hope to be; and on this rock we can also build our foreign policy.

185